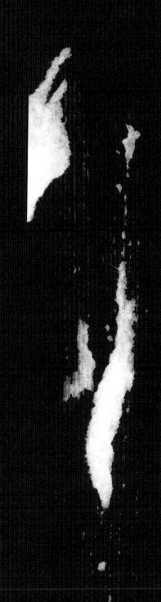

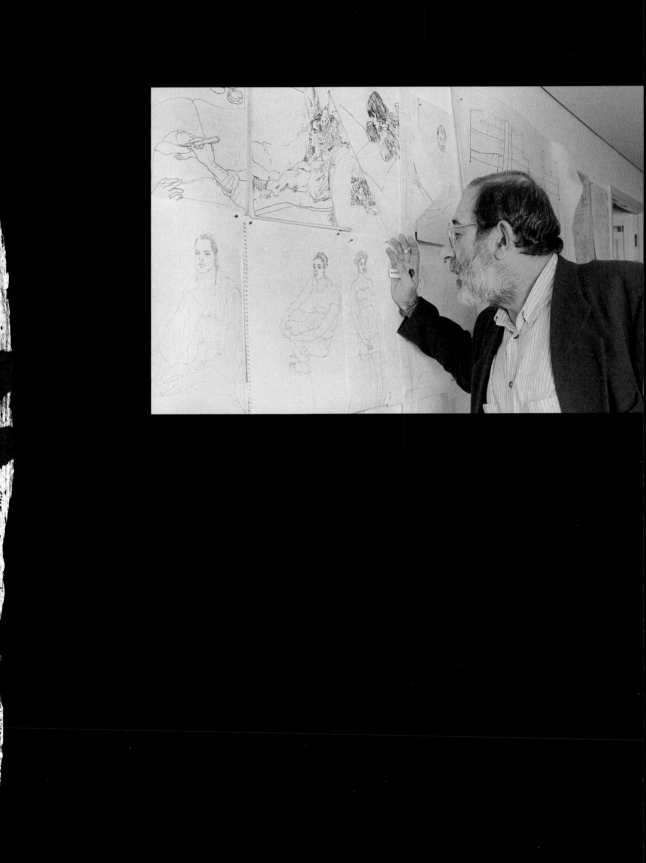

Álvaro

Siza

Philip Jodidio

TASCHEN

KÖLN LONDON LOS ANGELES MADRID PARIS TOKYO

Front cover > Couverture > Umschlagvorderseite
Borges & Irmão Bank, Vila do Conde, Portugal
© Photo: Hisao Susuki
Back cover > Dos de couverture > Umschlagrückseite
Portuguese Pavilion, Expo '98, Lisbon, Portugal
© Álvaro Siza
Page 1 > Seite 1
Portrait Álvaro Siza, 1993
Photo: Teresa Siza
Page 2 > Seite 2
Ocean Swimming Pool,
Leça da Palmeira, Portugal, 1961–1966
Photo: Hisao Suzuki

© 2003 TASCHEN GmbH
Hohenzollernring 53, D–50672 Köln
www.taschen.com

Originial edition: © 1999 Benedikt Taschen Verlag GmbH

Edited by Susanne Klinkhamels, Cologne
Co-edited by Christine Fellhauer, Cologne
Design: Quim Nolla [di'zain],
David Torrents and Adrià Nolla, Barcelona
French translation: Jacques Bosser, Paris
German translation: Annette Wiethüchter, Berlin

Printed in Italy
ISBN 3–8228–3011–9

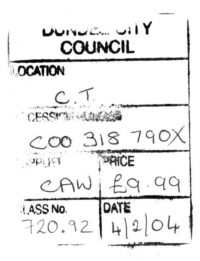

Contents > Sommaire > Inhalt

Winner of the Mies van der Rohe Prize (1988), the Pritzker Prize (1992), and the Praemium Imperiale (1998), Álvaro Siza Vieira clearly is a figure to be reckoned with. Born in 1933 in Matosinhos, on the outskirts of Porto, he is the best-known living Portuguese architect. His very personal blend of Modernist influences and direct responses to projects has given him an international stature that extends far beyond the limited number of buildings he has designed outside of Portugal. And yet the first contact with this unassuming chain-smoker belies the image of the "star" architect one might expect to encounter. In his old, cramped offices on the Rua da Alegria in Porto, Siza sits wherever there is a free space, between piles of drawings and models stacked one on top of another. Twenty architects work here, but Álvaro Siza gives the orders. There is no manager, no second in charge. Although he moved to more spacious purpose-built quarters on the Rua do Aleixo near the banks of the Douro in 1998, the old offices speak volumes about the style and method of Álvaro Siza.

Indeed the atmosphere in the Rua da Alegria offices was more like a busy artist's atelier than that of most international architectural practices. When asked if he considers himself an artist, Siza responds bluntly, "I would say that architecture is an art." This affirmation, tinged with a provocative touch, is quickly rationalized. "Architecture is becoming so hard. There are so many problems. It is not accepted as an art. It is almost taboo to say that architecture is an art. Today, quality in architecture often provokes a negative reaction. And so I have the need to stop sometimes and make drawings. I am also dangerously interested in sculpture. I know that Richard Meier sculpts. Others do as well. They probably feel the need to express themselves more freely than they can in architecture."

In some of his recent work, such as the Portuguese Pavilion at Expo '98 in Lisbon, Álvaro Siza has used his own drawings as a decor, for instance in the dining rooms. "Since I was a boy," he explains, "I have made drawings. I wanted to be a sculptor, but for

Lauréat du Prix Mies van der Rohe (1988), du Prix Pritzker (1992) et du Praemium Imperiale (1998), Álvaro Siza est à l'évidence une personnalité avec laquelle il faut compter. Né en 1933 à Matosinhos, dans la banlieue de Porto, il est le plus célèbre architecte portugais vivant. Son mariage très personnel d'influences modernistes et sa manière très directe de relever les défis que lui posent ses projets lui confèrent une stature internationale qui va bien au-delà du nombre limité de bâtiments qu'il a édifiés en dehors du Portugal. Le premier contact avec ce grand fumeur modeste ne correspond pas à l'image de star de l'architecture que l'on peut s'attendre à rencontrer. Dans son ancienne agence de la Rua da Alegria à Porto, il s'assoit là où il peut, entre des piles de dessins et des amoncellements de maquettes. 20 architectes travaillent ici, mais c'est Álvaro Siza qui commande. Il n'y a ni directeur d'agence ni second. Bien qu'il ait déménagé pour des bureaux plus spacieux qu'il a construits Rua do Aleixo au bord du Douro en 1998, son ancienne installation dit énormément sur son style et ses méthodes.

L'atmosphère de la Rua da Alegria fait davantage penser à un atelier d'artiste bourdonnant d'activité qu'à la plupart des agences internationales. Lorsqu'on lui demande s'il se considère comme un artiste, il répond froidement: «Je dis en effet que l'architecture est un art.» Cette affirmation, non sans un soupçon de provocation, est vite rationalisée: «L'architecture devient difficile. Il y a tant de problèmes. Elle n'est pas acceptée en tant qu'art. C'est presque toucher un tabou que de dire qu'elle est un art. Aujourd'hui, la qualité en architecture provoque souvent une réaction négative, et c'est pourquoi j'ai besoin parfois de m'arrêter et de dessiner. Je m'intéresse dangereusement de très près à la sculpture. Je sais que Richard Meier sculpte. D'autres aussi. Ils ressentent probablement un besoin de s'exprimer avec plus de liberté qu'en architecture.»

Dans certaines de ses œuvres récentes, comme le Pavillon du Portugal de l'Expo '98 à Lisbonne, Siza a utilisé ses propres

Architecture is an Art   L'architectu

Als Preisträger des Mies-van-der-Rohe-Preises (1988), des Pritzker-Preises (1992) und des japanischen Praemium Imperiale (1998) ist Álvaro Siza Vieira zweifellos eine bedeutende Persönlichkeit. Er wurde 1933 in Matosinhos bei Porto geboren und ist heute der weltweit bekannteste lebende portugiesische Architekt. Seine sehr persönliche Mischung aus Architekturmoderne und den spezifisch für jedes Projekt erarbeiteten Lösungen hat ihm eine internationale Anerkennung verschafft, die weit über die begrenzte Anzahl seiner außerhalb von Portugal realisierten Bauten hinausgeht. Dieser bescheiden auftretende Kettenraucher entspricht auf den ersten Blick in keiner Weise dem »Stararchitekten«, den man vielleicht erwartet. In seinen vollgestopften alten Büroräumen in der Rua da Alegria in Porto sitzt Siza da, wo er einen freien Platz gefunden hat: zwischen Stapeln von Bauzeichnungen und Architekturmodellen. 20 Architekten arbeiten hier, aber Álvaro Siza erteilt die Befehle. Das Büro hat keinen Manager, keinen zweiten Chef. Auch wenn Siza 1998 eigens für sein Architekturbüro erstellte neue, größere Räumlichkeiten in der Rua do Aleixo unweit des Douro-Flusses bezogen hat, sprechen die alten Räume Bände über den Stil und die Arbeitsmethoden von Álvaro Siza.

Tatsächlich wirken die Büros in der Rua da Alegria mehr wie ein geschäftiges Künstleratelier als die meisten Büros international tätiger Architekten. Auf die Frage, ob er sich selbst als Künstler sehe, antwortet Siza spontan: »Ich würde sagen, Architektur ist eine Kunst«, und liefert die Begründung für diese in leicht provokantem Ton geäußerte Behauptung: »Architektur [zu schaffen] wird immer schwerer. Es tauchen dabei so viele Schwierigkeiten auf. Sie wird nicht als Kunst anerkannt. Fast ist es tabu zu sagen, daß Architektur eine Kunst ist. Heutzutage ruft Qualität in der Architektur häufig eine negative Reaktion hervor. Deshalb muß ich manchmal eine Pause einlegen und freie Zeichnungen machen. Ich bin außerdem sehr an der Bildhauerei interessiert. Ich weiß, daß Richard Meier bildhauert, wie andere Architekten auch. Wahrscheinlich empfinden sie das Bedürfnis, sich freier auszudrücken, als das beim Bauen möglich ist.«

In mehreren seiner jüngsten Bauten – etwa dem portugiesischen Pavillon auf der Expo '98 in Lissabon – hat Álvaro Siza einige seiner künstlerischen Zeichnungen als dekorative Elemente verwendet, zum Beispiel in den Restaurants. »Schon als Junge habe ich gezeichnet«, sagt er. »Ich wollte Bildhauer werden, aber meine Eltern fanden das unrealistisch. Deshalb beschloß ich, mich an der Hochschule der bildenden Künste zu immatrikulieren, weil dort die drei Fächer Malerei, Bildhauerei und Architektur in den ersten zwei Studienjahren parallel gelehrt wurden. Ich hatte vor, später einfach das Fach zu wechseln, ohne mit meinen Eltern darüber zu diskutieren, aber dann faszinierte mich die Architektur doch zu sehr. Das Zeichnen – von Landschaften, Portraits, Reiseskizzen – hat mich in meiner Freizeit immer beschäftigt. Ich finde nicht, daß das freie Zeichnen einen direkten Bezug zur Architektur herstellt, aber es ist eine gute Methode, um den Blick zu schärfen. Das Portugiesische hat

my family that was not realistic. I decided to enter beaux arts school, where there were three courses – painting, sculpture, and architecture taught simultaneously in the first two years. My intention was to switch without discussing the matter with my family, but then I became deeply interested in architecture. Drawings – landscapes, portraits, and trip sketches – have always kept me busy. I don't think that it has a direct relation with architecture but it is a good way to develop acuity of vision. There are two different words in Portuguese that mean 'to look' and 'to see and understands' (olhar and ver). The tool of the architect is to be able to see. I remember reading a text by Alvar Aalto, where he wrote that, when a project was halted, that he would stop and just make drawings without a specific intention. Sometimes from this exercise, ideas would come to help move the project forward. There is a relation that is not direct."

Despite his deep commitment to architecture, Siza does seem to long for the freedom of art. When he says that architecture has become "hard" he affirms that it is not really a question of the commercial pressures placed on designers. "Architecture is related to business. That is normal," he declares. "There used to be an understanding, though, that business too needs quality. That is no longer the case. What counts is to be quick. It is normal in some European countries for the architect to make a design, and after that it goes to a promoter and a builder and they change whatever they want. It is felt that the architect is not necessary, and is not even allowed to go to the construction site. The relationship between designing and building, which is for me the same thing, is no longer maintained. To make a building it is necessary to have a complete team, acting like a single person, but today, all of the responsibility is broken up. This is what gives me the need to draw or to sculpt. In the end it is the same family of activities..."

In his built work, the artistic bent of Álvaro Siza appears not only in the occasional personal drawings that ornament a wall, but also in his remarkable attention to details – door handles, stair railings,

dessins comme décor, entre autres dans les salles à manger. «Depuis que je suis enfant, je dessine», explique-t-il, «je voulais devenir sculpteur, mais ce n'était pas un choix réaliste pour ma famille. J'ai décidé d'entrer à l'école des Beaux-Arts où trois cours – peinture, sculpture et architecture – étaient enseignés simultanément pendant les deux premières années d'étude. Mon intention était de faire mon choix sans en parler à ma famille, puis je me suis beaucoup intéressé à l'architecture. Les dessins – paysages, portraits et carnets de voyage – ont toujours beaucoup occupé mon temps. Je ne pense pas que cela ait une relation directe avec l'architecture, mais c'est une bonne façon de développer l'acuité d'une vision. En portugais, deux mots différents signifient ‹regarder› (olhar) et ‹voir et comprendre› (ver). L'outil de l'architecte est sa capacité à voir. Je me souviens d'un texte d'Alvar Aalto dans lequel il raconte que lorsqu'il se sentait bloqué sur un projet, il s'arrêtait et dessinait sans intention précise. Parfois, des idées naissaient de cet exercice qui permettaient de faire redémarrer le projet. La relation existe, mais n'est pas forcément directe.»

Malgré son profond engagement au service de l'architecture, Siza semble aspirer à la liberté artistique. Lorsqu'il dit que l'architecture est devenue «dure», il affirme que ce n'est pas vraiment le problème de la pression commerciale sur les créateurs. «L'architecture est liée aux affaires, c'est normal», déclare-t-il. «On a connu longtemps une compréhension mutuelle, car le monde des affaires a lui aussi besoin de qualité. Mais ce n'est plus le cas. Ce qui compte, c'est d'être rapide. On trouve normal dans certains pays européens que l'architecte dessine des plans qui sont ensuite transmis à un promoteur et à un constructeur qui les modifient comme ils veulent. On sent que l'architecte n'est plus nécessaire, et qu'il ne lui est même plus permis d'aller sur le chantier. La relation entre conception et construction, qui, pour moi, représentent la même chose, n'est plus préservée. Pour réaliser un bâtiment, il est nécessaire de

window closures, and a large variety of furniture. Why this emphasis on elements that can in good part be considered short-lived? "Ephemeral things are not dead things," maintains the architect. "They stay in the memory, or they influence somebody else. The destruction of something doesn't mean that it didn't exist; if we thought like that we would never make architecture, because we know very well that it will be altered and degraded with time." Perhaps the control that Siza exercises over his own office is reflected in this attention to detail. It would seem that he wishes to control everything in his buildings, down to the ashtrays. Siza contests that he feels he must be in total control, but admits that he does as much in his buildings as circumstances permit. "When we make a project," he says, "it seems obvious that the people who are going to live in it will probably be in another frame of mind. Of course we can give up, or say it is crazy to want to go further. I do not think so. In this meeting of different opportunities, and different cultural approaches, there is something for both sides. It is good for me too. I do not place myself in the position of saying that I am right and the others are wrong. I just try to meet them, to work together. In the case of the Portuguese Pavilion, I chose another architect, Eduardo Souto de Moura, to do a part of the interiors. My preoccupation is not to make everything. It is to find the way for the work to be born from a great variety of factors, some of which are in my mind – and others which are not."[1]

FROM MATOSINHOS TO ÉVORA

Álvaro Siza shares his new office building with a number of other Porto architects, including Eduardo Souto de Moura and Fernando Távora. Born in 1923, Távora has been a significant figure in Portuguese architecture since the early 1950s, teaching at the Porto School of Architecture (1953–93), where he pioneered an atmosphere of informal discussion in the classrooms. Having worked on such projects as the plan for the city center of Aveiro

disposer d'une équipe complète, qui travaille comme une seule entité. Aujourd'hui, cependant, toute la chaîne des responsabilités est rompue. C'est ce qui me donne envie de dessiner ou de sculpter. En final, c'est la même famille professionnelle.»

Les penchants artistiques de Siza apparaissent dans ses réalisations non seulement dans les quelques dessins qui ornent un mur à l'occasion, mais aussi dans le soin remarquable qu'il apporte aux détails – poignées de portes, rampes d'escalier, châssis de fenêtres, et une multiplicité de meubles de toute sorte. Pourquoi cet intérêt pour des éléments que l'on peut considérer pour une bonne part d'entre eux comme non durables? «Les choses éphémères ne sont pas des choses mortes», soutient l'architecte. «Elles restent dans la mémoire, ou influencent quelqu'un d'autre. La destruction de quelque chose ne signifie pas sa non-existence. Si nous pensions ainsi, nous ne ferions jamais d'architecture, car nous savons bien qu'elle sera altérée et dégradée avec le temps.»

Le contrôle que Siza exerce sur sa propre agence se reflète peut-être dans cette attention portée aux détails. Il semble qu'il veuille tout contrôler dans ses réalisations, jusqu'aux cendriers. Il conteste un goût du contrôle absolu, mais admet qu'il va aussi loin que les circonstances le permettent. «Lorsque nous préparons un projet, il nous semble évident que les gens qui viendront y vivre se trouveront vraisemblablement dans un autre état d'esprit que nous. Bien sûr, nous pourrions abandonner et penser qu'il serait stupide d'aller plus loin. Mais je ne le crois pas. Dans cette rencontre entre diverses opportunités et différentes approches culturelles, chacun peut trouver quelque chose. Cette remarque est également valable pour moi. Je ne me mets pas dans la position de dire que j'ai raison et que les autres ont tort. J'essaye simplement d'aller à leur rencontre, de travailler avec eux. Dans le cas du Pavillon du Portugal, j'ai choisi un autre architecte, Eduardo Souto de Moura, pour réaliser une partie des aménagements intérieurs. Ma préoccupation n'est pas de tout

zwei verschiedene Verben für ›sehen‹: Das eine bedeutet ›schauen/hinsehen‹ (olhar), das andere ›sehen und verstehen‹ (ver). Ein Werkzeug des Architekten ist sein Auge, sein scharfer Blick. Alvar Aalto hat einmal geschrieben, daß er – wenn er mit einem Entwurf nicht weiterkam – mit der Arbeit aufhörte und einfach zeichnete, ohne eine besondere Absicht zu verfolgen. Gelegentlich kamen ihm im Laufe dieser Übungen neue Ideen, die dazu beitrugen, das Bauprojekt weiter voranzutreiben. Es gibt also eine Beziehung, wenn auch keine direkte.«

Trotz seines intensiven Engagements als Architekt sehnt sich Siza offenbar nach der Freiheit der Kunst. Wenn er sagt, es sei schwierig geworden, Architektur zu schaffen, meint er nicht wirklich die Frage nach dem kommerziellen Druck auf den entwerfenden Architekten: »Bauen ist eine Wirtschaftstätigkeit. Das ist normal. Früher herrschte jedoch die Übereinkunft, daß auch das Geschäftemachen Qualität erfordert. Diesen Konsens gibt es heute nicht mehr. Interessant ist es, schnell zu sein. In einigen europäischen Ländern ist es inzwischen üblich, daß ein Architekt einen Entwurf abliefert, den dann der Bauträger und der Bauunternehmer nach Belieben abändern. Eigentlich hält man den Architekten für überflüssig, und man gestattet ihm noch nicht einmal den Zutritt zur Baustelle. Die direkte Verbindung zwischen Entwerfen und Bauen, die für mich eine Einheit bildet, besteht nicht mehr. Zum Bau eines Gebäudes braucht man ein Team, das wie eine einzelne Person handelt. Aber heute ist die Verantwortung auf viele verteilt. Deshalb brauche ich das freie Zeichnen oder die Bildhauerei. Schließlich gehört das alles zur gleichen Berufsfamilie...«

In seinen realisierten Bauten taucht Álvaro Sizas künstlerische Ader nicht nur in seinen als Wandornamente reproduzierten Zeichnungen auf, sie zeigt sich auch in der bemerkenswerten Sorgfalt, die er auf Details verwendet – Türgriffe, Treppengeländer, Fensterschließvorrichtungen und eine Vielzahl verschiedener Möbel. Warum diese Betonung von Elementen, die zum großen Teil als kurzlebig gelten? »Vergängliche Dinge sind lebendige Dinge«, meint der Architekt. »Sie bleiben im Gedächtnis haften oder beeinflussen andere. Wenn man ein Ding zerstört, heißt das nicht, daß es nie existiert hat. Wenn wir so dächten, würden wir keine Bauten mehr errichten, weil wir genau wissen, daß sie mit der Zeit umgebaut werden oder verfallen.«

Vielleicht spiegelt sich die Art von Kontrolle, die Siza über seine Mitarbeiter ausübt, in seiner Liebe zum Detail. Es scheint, als wolle er alles in seinen Gebäuden formen und bestimmen, bis hin zu den Aschenbechern. Siza bestreitet jedoch, daß er die totale Kontrolle ausüben will: »Wenn wir an einem Neubau arbeiten«, sagt er, »wissen wir ganz genau, daß die Menschen, die darin leben werden, wahrscheinlich eine ganz andere Denkweise haben als wir. Natürlich könnten wir aufgeben oder erklären, es sei verrückt weiterzumachen. Das finde ich nicht. Von diesem Zusammenkommen unterschiedlicher Möglichkeiten und kultureller Ansätze können beide Seiten profitieren. Das ist auch für mich gut. Ich versetze mich nicht in die Position desjenigen, der sagt, er habe recht und die anderen hätten

> Door and window handles designed
  by the architect.
> Poignées de portes et de fenêtres,
  conçues par l'architecte lui-même.
> Tür- und Fenstergriffe,
  vom Architekten selbst entworfen.

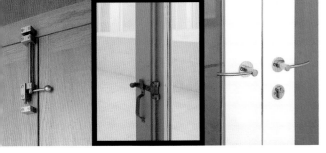

(1962–65), Távora is known for his desire to integrate traditional or local elements into a Modernist scheme. From 1955 to 1958 Siza worked with Fernando Távora, and it was Távora who chose the site on the Atlantic coast at Matosinhos near Porto where Siza was to build his first major project, the Boa Nova Tea House and Restaurant (Leça da Palmeira, 1958–63). Restored by Siza in 1991, this remarkable building is carefully integrated into an outcropping of rocks that at some points seem almost about to invade the interior space. A series of straight walls defines the space around the structure, leading the visitor to enter through a stairway, which offers an uninterrupted view of the sea. Although the site of the restaurant, now called the Casa de Chá, has an indisputable natural beauty, its increasingly urban environment on the inland side is quickly forgotten as one penetrates into the dark wood interior. A stairway leads down to the tearoom and restaurant, and in a gesture later seen to be typical of Siza's architecture, a window frames a view of the rocks. Another signature characteristic of Siza's work – his careful work on interior design and furniture – is here in full evidence. Although he may well have been influenced by Távora in this building, the Boa Nova Restaurant also brings to mind the designs of Frank Lloyd Wright.

Both the Boa Nova Restaurant and the nearby Ocean Swimming Pool (Leça da Palmeira, 1961–66) share a use by Siza of existing rock formations, a feature seen again in his Vieira de Castro House (Famalicão, 1984–98), yet he sees a distinct evolution in these two designs. As Álvaro Siza says, his approach to nature depends on circumstances. "What is made by men is not natural," he says. "More and more I think that there must be a certain distance between the natural and the man-made. But there must also be a dialog between the two. Architecture comes from natural forms, but it also transforms nature. If you look at the small restaurant I designed immediately before the swimming pool, there is a profile of rocks, and the building almost follows that

faire. C'est de trouver la manière de faire naître l'œuvre à partir d'une grande diversité de facteurs, dont certains m'appartiennent, et d'autres pas.»[1]

DE MATOSINHOS À ÉVORA

Álvaro Siza partage ses nouveaux bureaux avec plusieurs architectes de Porto, dont Eduardo Souto de Moura et Fernando Távora. Né en 1923, Távora est une personnalité qui compte dans l'architecture portugaise depuis le début des années 50 où, enseignant à l'École d'architecture de Porto (1953–93), il fut l'un des premiers à favoriser une atmosphère de discussion informelle pendant les cours. Responsable de projets comme le centre ville d'Aveiro (1962–65), il est connu pour intégrer des éléments traditionnels ou vernaculaires dans des plans d'esprit moderniste. C'est lui qui choisit le site de Matosinhos près de Porto, au bord de l'Atlantique, où Siza, son collaborateur de 1955 à 1958, édifia sa première réalisation notable, le restaurant et salon de thé Boa Nova (Leça da Palmeira, 1958–63). Restauré par Siza en 1991, ce remarquable bâtiment est soigneusement intégré à un affleurement rocheux qui, à certains endroits, semble presque envahir l'espace intérieur. Une succession de murs rectilignes définit l'espace tout autour de la construction, et oriente le visiteur vers l'escalier d'entrée qui offre une vue illimitée sur l'océan. Même si le site de ce restaurant, aujourd'hui appelé Casa de Chá, possède une indéniable beauté naturelle, son environnement de plus en plus urbanisé du côté des terres est vite oublié lorsque l'on pénètre dans son intérieur décoré de bois sombre. Un escalier descend vers le salon de thé et le restaurant, tandis que – dans un geste qui deviendra plus tard typique de l'architecture de Siza – une fenêtre cadre une vue sur les rochers. Une autre «signature» caractéristique du maître est le travail soigné de l'architecture intérieure et du mobilier, ici en évidence. S'il a pu être influencé par Távora, le restaurant Boa Nova fait également penser à certains projets de Frank Lloyd Wright.

Berlin
Ulli Stüd
Room

outline. Of course the swimming pool involved a longer, more horizontal space, but I tried to do a critique of my own approach in the restaurant. I thought the restaurant was too mimetical – it seems to be a part of the rocks in a way. In the swimming pool I designed five or six walls that relate to some of the rocks. The important thing is how this geometry encounters the natural elements, and how the landscape is transformed. I did not touch the rocks, I only added something recognizable as not natural. I put those things together; that is the way I see the relation between nature and architecture. If you look at the work of Frank Lloyd Wright, in his first phase he works with nature, but later on he works with the landscape. He transforms the natural environment. There is an affirmation of the built without ignoring the basic aspects of topography or the typology of the landscape."[2] Like the work of a number of modern architects, that of Álvaro Siza cannot necessarily be well understood through photographs. There is a subtlety in the effects of light that he orchestrates, and in the disposition of his architecture in its environment that the visitor feels but which cannot be rendered accurately by the camera. Thus, in the case of his swimming pool, the dark wood interiors of the changing rooms contrast with the band of bright daylight that he disposes at eye level. Outside, by integrating existing rocks into the forms of pools themselves, he makes visitors question their own sense of what is natural and what is built. In another remarkable gesture, he designs the main elevation of the changing areas, visible from the seaside, to look much like the cement retaining walls that run along the coast here. In a way, without adopting "too mimetical" a posture, he creates a modern design that blends into both its natural and its urban context.

One of the most ambitious projects of Álvaro Siza is his ongoing Quinta da Malagueira Social Housing located on the outskirts of Évora, 130 kilometers southeast of Lisbon. An important military post under the Romans, Évora was held by the Moors from 712 to

Le restaurant Boa Nova et la piscine voisine (Leça da Palmeira, 1961–66) possèdent en commun la mise à profit de formations rocheuses naturelles, que l'on retrouve également dans la maison Vieira de Castro (Famalicão, 1984–98), bien que l'on note une nette évolution entre ces deux projets. L'approche de la nature par Siza dépend des circonstances. «Ce qui est l'œuvre de l'homme n'est pas naturel», dit-il. «Je pense de plus en plus qu'il doit y avoir une certaine distance entre le naturel et ce qui est fait par l'homme. Mais le dialogue entre les deux est tout aussi nécessaire. L'architecture est issue de formes naturelles, mais elle transforme à son tour la nature. Si vous regardez ce petit restaurant que j'ai dessiné juste avant la piscine, on y aperçoit une ligne de rochers, dont le bâtiment suit presque le contour. Bien entendu, la piscine se devait d'occuper un espace plus long, plus horizontal, mais j'ai tenté une analyse critique de mon approche du restaurant. J'ai pensé qu'il était trop mimétique, qu'il semblait d'une certaine façon faire partie des rochers. Pour la piscine, j'ai dessiné cinq ou six murs en rapport avec quelques rochers. Ce qui compte, c'est la manière dont la géométrie se confronte avec les éléments naturels, et dont le paysage est transformé. Je n'ai pas touché aux rochers, j'ai seulement ajouté quelque chose que l'on puisse reconnaître comme non naturel. J'ai réunis ces éléments: c'est la façon dont je vois la relation entre la nature et l'architecture. Si vous regardez l'approche de Frank Lloyd Wright au cours de sa première phase, vous voyez qu'il travaille la nature, mais plus tard, qu'il intervient sur le paysage. Il transforme l'environnement naturel. Il y a chez lui une affirmation du bâti qui n'ignore pas les aspects essentiels de la topographie ou de la typologie du paysage.»[2]

Comme pour un certain nombre d'architectes modernes, l'œuvre d'Álvaro Siza est parfois difficile à bien percevoir à travers de simples photographies. La subtilité des effets de lumière qu'il orchestre et de l'implantation de son architecture dans l'environnement peut être ressentie par le visiteur, mais reste

unrecht. Ich versuche, ihnen entgegenzukommen, mit ihnen zusammenzuarbeiten. Im Fall des portugiesischen Expo-Pavillons beauftragte ich einen anderen Architekten, Eduardo Souto de Moura, damit, einen Teil der Innenräume zu gestalten. Mein Bestreben ist es gar nicht, immer alles selber zu machen. Ich will vielmehr eine Lösung finden, durch die das Bauwerk aus einer großen Vielfalt an Faktoren und Entwurfsideen erwächst, von denen einige meinem Kopf entspringen und andere nicht.«[1]

VON MATOSINHOS NACH ÉVORA

Álvaro Siza teilt sich sein neues Bürogebäude mit einer Reihe anderer Architekten, unter ihnen Eduardo Souto de Moura und Fernando Távora. Távora wurde 1923 geboren und ist seit Anfang der 50er Jahre ein bedeutender Vertreter der portugiesischen Architektur. Von 1953 bis 1993 war er Professor an der Hochschule für Architektur von Porto, wo er Seminare in Form von informellen Diskussionen einführte. Seit er Großprojekte wie den Generalplan für das neue Stadtzentrum von Aveiro (1962–65) erarbeitete, ist Távora für seine Bemühungen bekannt, traditionelle oder lokaltypische Stilelemente in eine insgesamt moderne Architektur zu integrieren. Von 1955 bis 1958 arbeitete Siza im Büro von Fernando Távora, und es war Távora, der das Baugrundstück an der Atlantikküste in Matosinhos bei Porto auswählte, auf dem Siza sein erstes größeres Gebäude erstellte: das Teehaus und Restaurant Boa Nova (Leça da Palmeira, 1958–63). Dieser bemerkenswerte Bau, den Siza 1991 renovierte, ist behutsam in einen Felsenvorsprung eingefügt, der an einigen Stellen fast in den Innenraum einzudringen scheint. Gerade Wände umschreiben den das Gebäude umgebenden Bereich und führen ankommende Besucher zum Eingang, und zwar über eine Treppe, von der aus sie freie Sicht auf das Meer haben. Die Lage des Restaurants (heute unter dem Namen Casa de Chá geführt) ist unbestreitbar von großer Naturschönheit. Sein zunehmend dicht bebautes Hinterland vergißt man schnell, wenn man das dunkel holzgetäfelte Innere betritt. Eine Treppe führt hinunter in das Teehaus und das Restaurant, und ein Fenster rahmt den Ausblick auf die Felsen ein – ein Element, daß später charakteristisch für Sizas Architektur sein wird. Ein anderes typisches Merkmal von Sizas Bauten ist hier augenfällig, nämlich die sorgfältig gestaltete Innenarchitektur und Möblierung. Obwohl sich Siza für diesen Bau wahrscheinlich von Távoras Architektur beeinflussen ließ, erinnert das Restaurant Boa Nova auch an die Entwürfe von Frank Lloyd Wright.

Sowohl beim Restaurant Boa Nova als auch beim nahegelegenen Meeresschwimmbad in Leça da Palmeira (1961–66) bezog Siza bestehende Felsformationen in die Baulichkeiten ein. Später griff er dieses Gestaltungsmittel für das Vieira de Castro Haus in Famalicão (1984–98) wieder auf, allerdings sieht er darin eine deutliche Weiterentwicklung der erstgenannten beiden Bauten. Sizas Umgang mit der Natur hängt nach eigener Aussage von den Umständen ab. »Die Schöpfungen der Menschen sind nicht natürlich«, meint er. »Ich komme immer mehr zu dem Schluß, daß es eine gewisse

> Boa Nova Tea House and Restaurant,
Leça da Palmeira, Portugal, 1958–63

1166. Still an agricultural trading center, it has a population of fewer than 40,000 persons, but boasts a walled inner city, which has been carefully preserved and includes the so-called Temple of Diana, a Roman structure dating from the first century A.D. Set to the west, outside the city walls, the Quinta da Malagueira includes 1,200 units of housing set on a site of 27 hectares. The finished parcels, separated by large green spaces, are defined by lots 11 by 8 meters in size. The variety of configurations in the housing units gives the whole an ordered yet varied appearance.

Begun over twenty years ago in 1977, the Quinta da Malagueira is not currently undergoing further development. When asked if it is finished, Siza replies, "No. In a way, nothing is ever finished. As long as they allow me to work there, I will do so. The development period was so long because of numerous problems, some of them political. The town has a Communist majority that is always opposed to the central government. In a country where the central government is so present, that makes financing difficult. Every four years at election time there are terrible attacks on the project from the local opposition. Recently, the Communist party lost its absolute majority in Évora, and the newspapers came out with articles calling my project crazy and monstrous – Stalinist even. The desire to remove me from the project was clearly expressed, and I do not know what will happen. What was built is far from what I initially projected. The financing came step by step for the housing, but for the town facilities things were much more complicated; there are other sources for this financing. You cannot really understand the overall atmosphere of the complex because you do not have the different scales that would be introduced by the planned public buildings for example. There are spaces that you cannot understand that are waiting for public buildings. I did not want to make a civic center. Of course, I am very much engaged in this project, but I do not know what will happen. In the center, where there is a square, there is to be a vault with a meeting place that is very important for the coherence of the

difficile à rendre sensible par la photographie. Ainsi, dans le cas de la piscine, les aménagements intérieurs des vestiaires en bois foncé contrastent avec le bandeau de lumière naturelle éblouissante qu'il a aménagé au niveau de l'œil. Au dehors, en intégrant les rochers existants dans les formes des bassins, il amène le visiteur à se poser des questions sur sa perception du naturel et du construit. Dans un autre geste étonnant, il conçoit l'élévation principale des vestiaires, visibles de la mer, de façon à ce qu'elle ressemble aux murs d'épaulement en ciment qui courent le long de la côte. À sa façon, sans adopter une posture «trop mimétique», il crée un design moderne qui se fond dans son contexte à la fois urbain et naturel.

L'un des plus ambitieux projets d'Álvaro Siza est son complexe de logements de la Quinta da Malagueira, dans la banlieue d'Évora, à 130 km au sud-est de Lisbonne. Importante place militaire sous les Romains, Évora est aux mains des Maures de 712 à 1166. Centre agricole important, elle possède aujourd'hui une population d'à peu près 40 000 habitants, et sa vieille ville entourée de remparts a été soigneusement préservée. Elle compte parmi ses monuments le temple dit de Diane, édifice romain du 1er siècle. Située à l'ouest, hors des remparts de la ville, la Quinta da Malagueira comprend 1 200 unités d'habitation sur un site de 27 hectares. Elles se trouvent sur des parcelles composées de lots de 11 x 8 mètres et entourées par de vastes espaces verts. La variété de configuration de ces maisons leur donne une apparence différenciée, mais ordonnée.

Lancé en 1977, ce projet est pour l'instant (1998) interrompu. À la question de savoir s'il est achevé, Siza répond: «Non. D'une certaine façon, rien n'est jamais fini. Aussi longtemps que l'on me permet de travailler ici, je le ferai. La période de développement a été longue parce que nous avons rencontré de multiples problèmes, dont certains politiques. La municipalité à majorité communiste s'est toujours opposée au gouvernement central. Dans un pays où celui-ci est très présent, cette attitude rend les

Distanz zwischen dem Natürlichen und dem von Menschenhand Geschaffenen geben muß, allerdings ebenso einen Dialog. Die Architektur entspringt natürlichen Formen, sie formt aber auch die Natur. Betrachtet man das Restaurant, das ich unmittelbar vor dem Meeresschwimmbad entworfen habe, sieht man eine Felsensilhouette, und das Haus folgt annähernd diesen Konturen. Natürlich erforderte das Strandbad längere, in der Horizontale angelegte Räume und Flächen, ich unternahm mit diesem Entwurf jedoch den Versuch, eine ›Rezension‹ meines eigenen Restaurantgebäudes zu realisieren. Ich fand das Restaurant inzwischen allzu mimetisch, da es in gewisser Weise Teil der Felsen zu sein scheint. Für das Schwimmbad sah ich fünf oder sechs Mauern vor, die auf einige der Felsblöcke Bezug nehmen. Wichtig ist, wie diese geometrischen Formen auf die natürlichen Elemente treffen und die Landschaft verwandeln. Ich ließ die Felsen völlig unangetastet und fügte nur etwas hinzu, das als nicht natürlich erkennbar ist. Ich habe beides zusammengefügt. So sehe ich das Verhältnis von Natur und Architektur. Wenn man sich das Werk von Frank Lloyd Wright anschaut, so fällt einem auf, daß er in der ersten Schaffensphase mit Natur arbeitet, später greift er in die Landschaft ein: Er verwandelt die natürliche Umgebung. Sein Werk ist eine Affirmation des Gebauten, ohne aber die grundlegenden Aspekte der Topographie oder des Landschaftstyps zu ignorieren.«[2]

Wie bei einer Reihe anderer moderner Architekten erschließen sich Álvaro Sizas Bauten dem Betrachter nur schwer, wenn er sie lediglich fotografiert sieht. Seine Lichteffekte und Lichtinszenierungen sind subtil, die Plazierung seiner Gebäude in ihrer topographischen Situation ist sorgfältig durchdacht. Der Besucher spürt dies, die Kamera aber kann es nicht adäquat wiedergeben. Bei seinem Meeresschwimmbad zum Beispiel bildet die Inneneinrichtung aus dunklem Holz in den Umkleideräumen einen starken Kontrast zum Fensterband auf Augenhöhe, durch das helles Tageslicht einfällt. Indem er in den Außenanlagen bestehende Felsen in die Schwimmbeckenformen integriert, bringt Siza die Besucher dazu, an ihrer eigenen Wahrnehmung von »natürlich« und »gebaut« zu zweifeln. Die vom Meer aus sichtbare Hauptfassade des Umkleidekabinenbereichs ist ein weiteres Element der architektonischen Gestaltung: Sie sieht aus wie eine der Betonstützmauern, die in dieser Gegend zur Uferbefestigung gebaut wurden. Ohne allzu mimetisch vorzugehen, hat Siza hier eine moderne Architektur geschaffen, die sich ebenso in die natürliche wie in die städtische Umgebung einfügt.

Eines von Álvaro Sizas ehrgeizigsten Bauprojekten ist die Wohnsiedlung Quinta da Malagueira am Stadtrand von Évora, ca. 130 Kilometer südöstlich von Lissabon. Évora war ein wichtiger Militärstützpunkt der Römer und von 712 bis 1166 unter maurischer Herrschaft. Évora ist auch heute noch ein Handelsplatz für landwirtschaftliche Produkte und hat knapp 40000 Einwohner. Die Stadt aber ist stolz auf ihre von alten Befestigungsmauern umgebene, sorgfältig restaurierte Altstadt mit ihrem römischen Tempel, dem sogenannten Diana-Tempel aus dem 1. Jahrhundert n. Chr. Westlich

whole project; the character of the town depends on the mixture of the different scales of public and private structures."

Although there were numerous protests against the walled nature of Siza's project in its early days, he pointed out himself that the city of Évora is itself walled. When asked today in this context whether his view of traditional Portuguese architecture and its influence on his own work has changed, he replies, "In my opinion it is not right to emphasize this vernacular influence in the design. With the economic constraints and the conditions in that area of Portugal, which is one of its less developed parts, you have to use traditional basic aspects for reasons of comfort. The white walls are there not only for aesthetic reasons related to the architecture of the south, but also to reflect the sun and give some thermal protection. The walls also exist in order to create a microclimate between the interior and the exterior, and not really as a vernacular image of a patio house. I read that there is a 'Neo-Rationalist' element to my architecture or a Bauhaus influence, but things don't work that way. I made the houses with cement-block walls because it was the material I could use there. I made terraces not only because of this image of Arab or Mediterranean housing but also because there was a lack of roofing tiles. The project was begun immediately after the Revolution, and at the time there was a boom in construction, and materials could not be found. We also had difficulty finding builders. Local builders had trouble with a program of 1,200 houses. This also explains why the inner town of Évora is so well preserved. These issues are important, and architectural criticism rarely deals with them."[3]

THE CHALLENGE OF NOTORIETY

Although he was well known in Portugal many years ago, Álvaro Siza's more recent jump to international recognition is in some ways related to the recent history of Portugal. As he has said, "It is natural that a typical case such as mine occurs in Portugal, which is a country that has traditionally been very isolated, even after the

financements délicats. Tous les quatre ans, au moment des élections, des attaques furieuses sont lancées contre le projet par l'opposition locale. Récemment, le parti communiste a perdu la majorité absolue, et les journaux ont qualifié mon projet de fou, de monstrueux, et même de stalinien. Le désir de m'écarter a été clairement exprimé, et je ne sais pas ce qui va se passer. Ce qui a été construit est loin de ce que j'avais projeté au départ. Le financement est venu par étape pour les logements, mais les choses ont été beaucoup plus compliquées pour les équipements urbains, car les fonds venaient d'autres sources. Par exemple, on ne peut vraiment comprendre l'atmosphère générale de l'ensemble, car les différences d'échelle doivent être introduites par des bâtiments publics qui n'existent toujours pas. Certains espaces sont incompréhensibles sans les bâtiments prévus pour eux. Je ne voulais pas de centre municipal. Bien entendu, je reste très engagé dans ce projet, mais je ne sais pas ce qu'il va devenir. Au centre, là où se trouve une place, il devrait y avoir une grande halle voûtée et un point de rencontre très important pour la cohérence de la totalité de l'ensemble. Le caractère de la ville dépendra des différences d'échelle entre les constructions publiques et privées.»

Bien que de nombreuses protestations se soient élevées contre l'aspect «emmuré» du projet à ses débuts, Siza fait remarquer qu' Évora elle-même est une cité entourée de murailles. Lorsqu'on lui demande aujourd'hui dans ce contexte si sa vision de l'architecture traditionnelle portugaise et de son influence sur son propre travail a changé, il répond: «À mon sens, il n'est pas juste de mettre l'accent sur cette influence vernaculaire dans ce projet. Dans le cadre des contraintes économiques et des conditions de vie dans cette région, qui est l'une des moins développées du Portugal, vous devez tenir compte de certains aspects traditionnels ne serait-ce que pour des raisons de confort. Les murs blancs ne sont pas là que pour de simples motifs esthétiques qui relèveraient d'une architecture du sud, mais pour

der Stadtmauern entsteht die Wohnsiedlung Quinta da Malagueira mit 1200 Wohneinheiten auf einem 27 Hektar großen Gelände. Die fertiggestellten Häuser stehen auf 11 x 8 Meter großen Grundstücken, umgeben von großzügigen Grünflächen. Die unterschiedlichen Formen der Wohneinheiten sorgen für das geordnete und zugleich abwechslungsreiche Erscheinungsbild der Siedlungsanlage.

Mit dem Bau von Quinta da Malagueira wurde 1977 begonnen. Derzeit wird nicht weiter daran gebaut. Auf die Frage, ob die Siedlung fertiggestellt ist, antwortet Siza immer: »Nein. In gewisser Weise wird nichts jemals fertig. Solange sie mir erlauben, dort weiter zu arbeiten, werde ich es tun. Die Bauzeit hat sich deshalb so in die Länge gezogen, weil sich zahlreiche Schwierigkeiten ergaben, zum Teil politischer Art. Die Stadtregierung ist mehrheitlich kommunistisch und opponiert gegen die Zentralregierung. In einem Land, in dem die Zentralregierung so allgegenwärtig ist wie in Portugal, erschwert das die Finanzierung. Alle vier Jahre zur Zeit der Wahlen wird das Siedlungsprojekt von der lokalen Opposition heftig attackiert. Vor kurzem haben die Kommunisten ihre absolute Mehrheit in Évora verloren, und in den Zeitungen erschienen Artikel, in denen mein Projekt verrückt und monströs geschimpft wurde – ja sogar ›stalinistisch‹. Ganz offen wurde gefordert, mir das Bauvorhaben zu entziehen, und ich weiß nicht, was passieren wird. Was tatsächlich gebaut wurde, ist weit entfernt von meinem ursprünglichen Entwurf. Die Finanzierung der Wohnbauten wurde Schritt für Schritt bewilligt, für die öffentlichen Einrichtungen war der Prozeß jedoch wesentlich komplizierter, weil die Gelder aus anderen Quellen fließen mußten. Zur Zeit kann man die Atmosphäre und Form des Gesamtkomplexes noch gar nicht erfassen, weil der Maßstabsvergleich mit den geplanten öffentlichen Gebäuden nicht möglich ist. Es gibt Freiflächen, die keinen Sinn machen, weil sie noch auf ihre Bebauung mit öffentlichen Einrichtungen warten. Ich wollte die öffentlichen Einrichtungen nicht zentral gruppieren. Natürlich engagiere ich mich sehr für dieses Siedlungsvorhaben, aber ich weiß nicht, wie sich die Dinge entwickeln werden. Im Zentrum, wo sich ein öffentlicher Platz befindet, soll ein Gewölbe mit einem Begegnungsort entstehen, der für den Zusammenhalt des ganzen Komplexes sehr wichtig ist. Der Charakter des Stadtteils hängt von der Mischung ab, von den unterschiedlichen Maßstäben öffentlicher und privater Gebäude.«

Als Sizas Projekt noch in den Anfängen steckte, gab es zahlreiche Proteste gegen seinen von Mauern bestimmten Charakter; Siza wies aber darauf hin, daß die Stadt Évora selbst von Stadtmauern umfaßt wird. Wenn er in diesem Zusammenhang heute danach gefragt wird, ob sich seine Sicht auf die traditionelle portugiesische Architektur und ihr Einfluß auf sein Werk geändert hat, antwortet er: »Meiner Meinung nach ist es falsch, diesen lokaltypischen Einfluß auf den Entwurf zu betonen. Bei allen wirtschaftlichen Zwängen und den Zuständen in jener Gegend Portugals, die zu den rückständigsten des Landes gehört, muß man aus Gründen des Komforts bestimmte grundlegende traditio-

Second World War. Leaving the country was severely controlled, information was regulated, there was a lot of censorship; the opening up began in the 1960s, and accelerated after the 'Revolution dos Claveles' ('Revolution of the Carnations') in 1974, bringing about great curiosity and an urgent need for contact. The condition of distance was a stimulus to learn and construct an architecture capable of exiting from the strictly local scene, of becoming more universal..." As Siza says, "Universality is not equivalent to neutrality, it is not the Esperanto of architectural expression, it is the capacity to create from the roots. My sense of universality has more to do with the vocation of the cities, arising from centuries of intervention, of crossbreeding, of superposition and mixing of the most opposed influences, creating however an unmistakable identity."[4]

It was a bloodless military coup on May 28, 1926, that instituted what was to become western Europe's most long-lived authoritarian system. At first named Minister of Finance by General António Oscar de Fragoso Carmona, António de Oliveira Salazar, previously a professor of economics at the University of Coimbra, became Prime Minister of Portugal in July 1932, a post that he held until 1968. Six years later, a group of about 250 military officers headed by Francisco da Costa Gomes planned and implemented the coup of April 25, 1974, which came to be known as the "Revolution of the Carnations" because it occurred during the week that red carnations appeared in the flower shops.

The decolonization of the former Portuguese colonies in Africa (Mozambique, Angola, and Guinea-Bissau) led to the repatriation of nearly a million persons, but since that time Portugal has worked something of an economic miracle. With a high economic growth rate (currently 3.8%), low inflation (2.2%), and relatively low unemployment (6.8%), Portugal qualified easily in March 1998 to join the eleven countries that will adopt the euro as their currency in 2002. This climate of growth also has something to do with the emergence on the international scene of Álvaro Siza.

refléter le soleil et offrir une certaine protection thermique. Les murs ont aussi pour fonction de créer un microclimat entre l'intérieur et l'extérieur, et non pour évoquer la maison à patio vernaculaire. J'ai lu que l'on trouvait un élément ‹néo-rationaliste› ou Bauhaus dans mon architecture, mais les choses ne fonctionnent pas ainsi. J'ai construit ces maison avec des murs en blocs de ciment parce que c'était le matériau que je pouvais utiliser ici. J'ai dessiné ces terrasses non seulement par référence à des influences arabes ou méditerranéennes, mais aussi parce que l'on trouvait difficilement des tuiles. Le projet a été lancé immédiatement après la Révolution. À l'époque, il y avait un boom de la construction et l'on ne trouvait plus de matériaux. Nous avons eu également des problèmes pour trouver des constructeurs. Les locaux avaient des difficultés à traiter un programme de 1 200 maisons. Ceci explique également pourquoi la vieille ville d'Évora est si bien protégée. Ces problèmes sont importants et la critique architecturale en tient rarement compte.»[3]

LE DÉFI DE LA NOTORIÉTÉ

Bien que Siza soit très connu au Portugal depuis de longues années, son accès récent à la célébrité internationale est d'une certaine façon liée à l'histoire contemporaine de ce pays. Comme il l'a déclaré: «Il est caractéristique qu'un cas comme le mien puisse se produire au Portugal, nation traditionnellement très isolée, même après la Seconde Guerre mondiale. Il était alors très difficile de quitter le pays, l'information était contrôlée, et la censure très présente. L'ouverture a commencé dans les années soixante, et s'est accélérée après la Révolution des œillets en 1974, entraînant beaucoup de curiosité et un impérieux besoin de contacts. L'éloignement était le stimulus qui nous poussait à apprendre et à construire une architecture capable d'exister en dehors d'un contexte purement local et de devenir plus universelle. L'universalité n'est pas l'équivalent de la neutralité, ce n'est pas l'espéranto de l'expression architecturale, c'est la

nelle Aspekte berücksichtigen. Die Mauern sind nicht nur aus ästhetischen Gründen weiß – um als Architektur des Südens zu wirken –, sondern auch um das Sonnenlicht zu reflektieren und Sonnenwärme abzustrahlen. Die Mauern sind auch dazu da, ein Mikroklima zwischen Innen und Außen zu schaffen, und sind nicht eigentlich ein lokaltypisches Bild eines Patio-Haustyps. Ich lese, daß es in meiner Architektur ›neo-rationalistische‹ Elemente oder Bauhaus-Einflüsse gibt, aber so funktioniert das nicht. Ich sah für die Häuser deshalb Zementwerksteinmauern vor, weil sich dieses Baumaterial hier als geeignet anbot. Ich entwarf Dachterrassen nicht nur, weil arabische oder mediterrane Häuser eben Dachterrassen haben, sondern auch, weil nicht genügend Dachziegel vorhanden waren. Die Bauarbeiten wurden sofort nach der Revolution in Angriff genommen, als ein Bauboom herrschte und es kaum Baumaterialien gab. Wir hatten auch Schwierigkeiten, einen Bauunternehmer zu finden. Die lokalen Firmen waren mit einem Neubauprogramm von 1200 Häusern überfordert. Das erklärt auch, warum die Altstadt von Évora so gut erhalten ist. Diese Aspekte sind wichtig, aber kaum eine Architekturkritik befaßt sich mit ihnen.«[3]

INTERNATIONALES RENOMMEE ALS HERAUSFORDERUNG

Obwohl Álvaro Siza in Portugal schon vor vielen Jahren bekannt war, hat sein plötzlicher Aufstieg in die Riege international anerkannter Architekten in jüngster Zeit in gewisser Hinsicht mit den neuen politischen Entwicklungen seines Heimatlandes zu tun. Wie er selbst sagt, ist es »natürlich, daß solch ein typischer Fall wie meiner in Portugal passiert, einem Land, das traditionell sehr isoliert gewesen ist, selbst nach dem Zweiten Weltkrieg. Auslandsreisen wurden streng überwacht, Informationen kanalisiert, vieles wurde zensiert. Die Öffnung des Landes begann in den 6oer Jahren und beschleunigte sich nach der ›Nelkenrevolution‹ von 1974, die einen großen Wissensdurst und ein zwingendes Bedürfnis nach Kontakten mit dem Ausland nach sich zog. Der Zustand der Isolation und Distanz weckte den Impuls, Neues zu lernen und eine Architektur zu schaffen, die in der Lage war, aus der strikt örtlichen Situation herauszutreten, universaler zu werden. Universalität ist nicht gleichbedeutend mit Neutralität. Sie ist nicht das Esperanto des architektonischen Ausdrucks, sondern die Fähigkeit, aus den Wurzeln zu schöpfen. Mein Verständnis von Universalität hat eher mit der Berufung und Bestimmung von Städten zu tun, die aufgrund von jahrhundertelangen Eingriffen, Kreuzungen, Überlagerungen und unterschiedlichsten Prägungen gewachsen sind und dadurch eine unverwechselbare Identität gewonnen haben.«[4]

Es war ein unblutiger Militärputsch, der am 28. Mai 1926 in Portugal eine Regierung an die Macht brachte, die in der Folge eines der langlebigsten autoritären Systeme in Westeuropa bilden sollte. António de Oliveira Salazar, bis dahin Professor für Wirtschaftswissenschaften an der Universität Coimbra, wurde von General António Carmona 1928 zum Finanzminister ernannt und war später,

Portuguese Pavilion, Expo '98, Lisbon, Portugal, 1995–98.
> One of the restaurants of the Pavilion, on the upper level.
> L'un des restaurants du Pavillon, à l'étage supérieur.
> Eines der Restaurants des Pavillons im Obergeschoß.

Three university projects designed and completed by Álvaro Siza between the late 1980s and the mid-1990s do much to cast light on the richness and complexity of his design work. The first of these to be completed, the Faculty of Architecture at the University of Porto (1987–93), is in a sense the most significant, if only because it involves Siza's own alma mater and the school where he has taught. Set high above the estuary of the Douro River, which crosses Porto, the Faculty is divided into a number of pavilions, which are interconnected both above and, for a number of them, below ground. The largest structure, the north wing, forms the inner limit of the internal triangular courtyard and contains offices, auditoriums, a semicircular exhibition space that has yet to be used, and a library with a surprising hanging skylight that pierces through its roof. The pavilions on the side of the Douro are each different and contain classrooms. The outer facades of these structures have decidedly anthropomorphic features, a recurrent element of many but not all of Siza's designs. Some, including members of the Porto Faculty, criticize Siza for the relatively small size of the classrooms and the pavilions of this facility, accusing him of wishing to impose his idea of restricted class groups. Siza replies to this critique in typically straightforward fashion: "The design of the four towers takes into account the idea that the students should have different views out the windows in each classroom. There are many other reasons for the pavilions. I wanted to open the school toward the river. I wanted to create a clear central space, but also to relate the buildings to the existing houses near the site. I was given a program that was prepared by the Ministry. It provided for 500 students and fifteen groups of fifteen students. I could not change this. I was obliged to work exactly on the number of square meters provided for in the program. I questioned the lack of flexibility, but I was told it would be like that. They also imposed a maximum area of 30% for corridors and other gathering places. I fought hard to come up to 40%. I did not succeed, and that is a big mistake."

capacité de créer à partir de racines. Mon sens de l'universel a davantage de rapports avec la vocation des villes, nées de siècles d'interventions, de croisements, de superpositions et du mélange des influences les plus opposées, tout en créant une identité évidente.»[4] C'est par un coup d'État militaire et sans qu'une seule goutte de sang ne soit versée, le 28 mai 1926, que s'instaura ce qui allait devenir le régime autoritaire le plus long qu'ait connu l'Europe occidentale au XXe siècle. Nommé ministre des finances par le général António Carmona, António de Oliveira Salazar, professeur d'économie à l'Université de Coimbra, devint premier ministre du Portugal en juillet 1932, poste qu'il conserva jusqu'en 1968. Six ans plus tard, un groupe de 250 officiers sous la direction de Francisco da Costa Gomes réussit le soulèvement du 25 avril 1974, appelé depuis la «Révolution des œillets», car il se déroula au cours de la semaine où les œillets rouges apparaissent chez les fleuristes.

La décolonisation des anciens territoires portugais d'Afrique (Mozambique, Angola et Guinée-Bissau) contraignit au rapatriement de près d'un million de personnes. Depuis, le Portugal a accompli une sorte de miracle économique. Avec un taux de croissance élevé (actuellement 3,8%), une inflation réduite (2,2%) et un taux de chômage relativement faible (6,8%), il a pu faire partie sans trop de difficultés du groupe de pays qui adopteront l'euro en 2002. Ce climat favorable n'est pas sans rapport avec l'émergence d'Álvaro Siza sur la scène internationale. Trois projets d'universités conçus et menés à bien par Siza de la fin des années 80 au milieu des années 90 ont attiré l'attention sur la richesse et la complexité de son œuvre. La première achevée, la faculté d'architecture de l'Université de Porto (1987–93), est, en un sens, la réalisation la plus significative, ne serait-ce que parce qu'elle concerne l'école où Siza a étudié et enseigné. Située au-dessus de l'estuaire du Douro qui traverse Porto, elle se répartit en un certain nombre de pavillons reliés par des passerelles ou des souterrains. La plus vaste construction,

> Vieira de Castro House, Famalicão, Portugal, 1984–98

A school needs open spaces for meetings and communication. I understand that there are problems with money, but the money spent on education reproduces itself a thousand times."[5]

A second major university project by Álvaro Siza is his Superior School of Education in Setúbal (1986–94). Located on the northern shore of the estuary formed by the Sado, Marateca, and São Martinho rivers, Setúbal is Portugal's third largest port. A description by the Portuguese critic Madalena Cunha Matos gives some idea of the slight impression of unease that seems to permeate a basically quite classical layout. "This is an intriguing work. Because of its extreme beauty, albeit a beauty in which disorder shows through, beyond and beneath the calm. Because of the confusion its very existence unleashes... In stark contrast to the whiteness, number and reason, forms emerge that are negative, threatening: a sombre face anthropomorphically designed on the façade of a projecting staircase; a slowly uncurling sea creature that might at any moment retreat back into its shell, closing off access to the interior; a structural collapse, freeze-framed in a given moment of its fall; the inescapable presence in the background of two towering stacks, factory chimneys vomiting forth their black, soon-to-be-breathed smoke; the contorted, knotted branches of a cork tree rising to meet the sky."[6]

It has been suggested that Siza conscientiously planned the design of the Setúbal structure around the very tree mentioned in this description, but here again, his own words more accurately describe the actual chain of events: "That site was full of trees, but we had to cut some of them to build the structure. I said that the trees that could be saved should be. They finished cutting, and I saw that this tree was exactly in the center of the space. I said that this was a miracle. I probably would have put a new one there if the old one did not exist. Everybody thinks that I designed the building to maintain that tree in the center. No, it was just lucky that it was there."[7]

l'aile nord, forme la limite septentrionale intérieure de la cour triangulaire intérieure et contient des bureaux, des auditoriums, un espace d'exposition semi-circulaire qui n'a pas encore trouvé d'emploi, et une bibliothèque à l'étonnante verrière suspendue qui traverse le toit. Les pavillons sur la rive du Douro sont tous différents et abritent des salles de cours. Leurs façades extérieures présentent des traits résolument anthropomorphiques, élément récurrent dans beaucoup de projets de Siza.

Certains, dont quelques membres de la faculté de Porto, critiquent Siza pour la taille relativement réduite des salles de cours et des pavillons, l'accusant de vouloir imposer sa conception d'un enseignement par petits groupes. Il réplique à cette critique à sa manière habituelle, très directement: «La conception des quatre blocs a pris en compte l'idée que les étudiants devaient pouvoir bénéficier de vues différentes à travers les fenêtres de chaque salle. Beaucoup d'autres raisons expliquent les pavillons. Je voulais ouvrir l'école vers le fleuve. Je souhaitais également créer un espace central clair, mais aussi relier les bâtiments aux maisons voisines existantes. On m'a donné un programme préparé par le ministère. Il correspondait à 500 étudiants et 15 groupes de 15 étudiants, et je ne pouvais pas le modifier. J'étais obligé de travailler sur le nombre de mètres carrés précis prévu par le programme. J'ai remis en question le manque de souplesse, mais on m'a répondu que l'on ne pouvait rien y faire. On m'a également imposé une surface maximum de 30% pour les circulations et lieux de rencontre. Je me suis battu pour obtenir 40%. Je n'ai pas réussi, et c'est certainement une grave erreur. Une école a besoin d'espaces ouverts pour les rencontres et la communication. Je comprends qu'il y ait eu des problèmes d'argent, mais l'argent dépensé dans l'éducation se multiplie mille fois par lui-même.»[5]

Le second grand projet universitaire de Siza est l'École normale supérieure de Setúbal (1986–94). Située sur la rive nord de l'estuaire du Sado, la ville est le troisième plus grand port du pays.

von Juli 1932 bis 1968, Portugals Ministerpräsident. Sechs Jahre nach seiner Ablösung, am 25. April 1974, führte eine Gruppe von etwa 250 Armeeoffizieren unter Führung von Francisco da Costa Gomes einen Staatsstreich durch, der als »Nelkenrevolution« in die Geschichte einging, weil er in der Woche geschah, als die ersten roten Nelken in den Blumenläden verkauft wurden.

Die Auflösung der ehemals portugiesischen Kolonien in Afrika (Moçambique, Angola und Guinea-Bissau) in den 70er Jahren führte zur Heimkehr von fast einer Million Portugiesen ins Mutterland. Seither hat Portugal eine Art Wirtschaftswunder zustande gebracht. Mit seiner hohen Wirtschaftswachstumsrate (3,8%), niedrigen Inflation (2,2%) und einer relativ geringen Arbeitslosigkeit (6,8%) qualifizierte sich Portugal im März 1998 mühelos für den Beitritt zur Gruppe der elf europäischen Länder, die im Jahr 2002 den Euro als gemeinsame Währung haben werden. Dieses Wachstumsklima hat auch dazu beigetragen, daß Álvaro Siza in den letzten Jahren in der internationalen Architekturszene bekannt geworden ist.

Drei Universitätsgebäude, die Álvaro Siza Ende der 80er bis Mitte der 90er Jahre entworfen und realisiert hat, eignen sich vor allen anderen seiner Werke dazu, die Vielfalt und Komplexität seiner Architektur zu beleuchten. Das erste fertiggestellte Gebäude der Architekturfakultät der Universität Porto (1987–93) ist in gewissem Sinne das bedeutendste, schon aufgrund der Tatsache, daß es zu Sizas eigener Alma Mater gehört, an der er später selber lehrte und noch lehrt. Hoch über der Mündung des Douro gelegen, der die Stadt Porto durchzieht, besteht das Fakultätsgebäude aus mehreren Pavillons, die miteinander verbunden sind (zum Teil unterirdisch). Der größte Bauteil ist der Nordflügel. Er bildet die nördliche Begrenzung des innenliegenden, dreieckigen Patios und enthält Büros, Hörsäle, einen halbrunden Ausstellungsraum (der bislang ungenutzt ist) und eine Bibliothek mit einer ungewöhnlichen, herabhängenden Oberlichtkonstruktion, die das Dach durchstößt. Die Pavillons zum Fluß hin sind alle verschieden und beherbergen Seminarräume. Ihre Außenfassaden tragen deutlich anthropomorphe Züge, ein Gestaltungsmittel, das in vielen Bauten von Siza wiederkehrt. Einige Kritiker – unter ihnen Mitglieder des Lehrkörpers der Architekturfakultät – bemängeln die relativ kleinen Abmessungen der Unterrichtsräume und der Pavillons insgesamt. Sie werfen Siza vor, er wolle der Fakultät dadurch seine Vorstellung von kleinen Studentengruppen aufzwingen. Siza weist diesen Vorwurf in seiner typisch direkten Art zurück: »Der Entwurf der vier Turmhäuser berücksichtigt den Gedanken, daß die Studenten von jedem Unterrichtsraum aus verschiedene Ausblicke aus den Fenstern haben sollten. Es gibt viele Gründe für den Pavillontyp: Zum einen wollte ich das Fakultätsgebäude zum Fluß hin öffnen, zum anderen einen klar umrissenen zentralen Raum schaffen, und außerdem die Gebäude zum umgebenden Baubestand in Bezug setzen. Das Ministerium lieferte das Bauprogramm, das Raumbedarf für 500 Studenten und 15 Gruppen mit je 15 Studenten vorsah. Diese Vorgaben durfte ich nicht ändern. Ich war gezwungen, exakt die Anzahl Quadratmeter

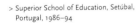

> Superior School of Education, Setúbal,
  Portugal, 1986–94

The question of the architectural influences that have formed the style of Álvaro Siza is often evoked. In the case of a building such as that in Setúbal, the names of Adolf Loos or Luis Barragán are evoked frequently. Another university building by Siza brings to mind an even more explicit reference. His Library of the University of Aveiro (1988–95) is one of his most complete and successful works. Located in the midst of a modern university, the building adopts a brick cladding and limestone trim that were dictated by the building codes of the institution. Here almost every detail, from the handrails for the stairs to the counters, which are cantilevered forward, and every light fixture in the building, is designed by Siza himself. Windows offer carefully framed views onto the neighboring marshland, recalling early work of Siza's such as the Boa Nova restaurant, but also more recent designs such as his church in Marco. On the west side of the building facing the marshes, an undulating brick wall definitely brings to mind the House of Culture by Alvar Aalto (Helsinki, Finland, 1952–58), while the interior space might recall his dining hall and lounge of Baker House, a dormitory at MIT (Cambridge, Massachusetts, 1946–49) or Aalto's Mount Angel Abbey Library (St. Benedict, Oregon, 1964–70). When asked today to comment on the influence of Aalto on his work, Siza replies, "In the 1950s in Italy, Spain, and Portugal, Aalto had a great influence. There are two reasons for this. In the ambiance of postwar architecture, the reconstruction of Europe was handled in an industrial manner in France, Germany, or the Netherlands. Countries on the periphery, such as Portugal, were not as industrialized. In Portugal or Spain there were common points with Finland. In Finland, it was difficult to obtain cement, but artisans able to work wood, for example, were available. Alvar Aalto became a very important reference. Aalto came many times to Spain and North Africa and Greece, and also a bit to Portugal. He brought many of these elements of the architecture of these areas to Finland. There were relations and influences that had an effect on my school when I

La description inattendue qu'en fournit la critique portugaise Madalena Cunha Mathos donne une certaine idée de la légère impression de malaise qui semble émaner de ce plan assez classique: «C'est un travail intriguant», dit-elle, «du fait de son extrême beauté, bien qu'une beauté à travers laquelle transparaît le désordre, sous et à travers le calme. En contraste marqué avec toute cette blancheur émergent des formes négatives, menaçantes: un faciès sombre et anthropomorphique dessiné sur la façade d'une cage d'escalier en projection, une créature marine qui se déroule lentement et pourrait à chaque instant rentrer dans sa coquille en fermant tout accès à l'intérieur, un effondrement structurel, gelé dans sa chute, ou encore la présence incontournable dans le fond de deux sortes de cheminées d'usine vomissant au loin une fumée noire que l'on risquerait de respirer, ou les branches contournées et noueuses d'un chêne-liège qui tentent de monter vers le ciel.»[6]

On a pu suggérer que Siza avait consciemment planifié le dessin de son projet de Setúbal autour de l'arbre qu'il mentionne dans sa description, mais il faut écouter de sa propre bouche la chaîne chronologique des éléments: «Ce terrain était couvert d'arbres, mais il a fallu en abattre un certain nombre pour pouvoir construire. J'ai demandé que l'on en sauve autant que possible. Après la coupe, j'ai réalisé que cet arbre se trouvait exactement au centre de l'espace. J'ai pensé que c'était un miracle. J'en aurais probablement fait planter un autre s'il n'avait pas existé. Tout le monde pense que j'ai dessiné ce bâtiment pour maintenir cet arbre au centre. Non, c'était juste une chance qu'il soit là.»[7] La question des influences architecturales qui ont contribué à la formation du style de Siza est souvent cités. Dans le cas de bâtiments comme celui de Setúbal, les noms d'Adolf Loos ou de Luis Barragán sont fréquemment cités. Un autre bâtiment universitaire fournit une référence encore plus explicite: la bibliothèque de l'Université d'Aveiro (1988–95), l'une de ses œuvres les plus achevées et les plus réussies. Implanté au milieu

einzuhalten, die im Programm festgeschrieben waren. Ich wies auf den Mangel an Flexibilität hin, aber es hieß dann: So ist es eben. Für Korridore und andere Gemeinschaftsflächen war auch ein Maximum von 30% der Gesamtfläche vorgeschrieben. Ich kämpfte darum, bis zu 40% einplanen zu dürfen, leider erfolglos, und das ist ein großes Manko. Eine Lehranstalt braucht große freie Räume für Begegnung und Kommunikation. Ich verstehe ja, daß die öffentlichen Mittel knapp sind, aber das Geld, das man ins Bildungswesen steckt, vervielfältigt sich später doch tausendfach.«[5]

Ein weiteres großes Universitätsgebäude von Álvaro Siza ist das Ausbildungsinstitut für Lehrer in Setúbal (1986–94). Die Stadt Setúbal liegt an der breiten Mündungsbucht des Sado und besitzt Portugals drittgrößten Hafen. Eine Baubeschreibung von Madalena Cunha Matos, einer portugiesischen Kunstkritikerin, vermittelt einen Eindruck der leichten Unruhe, die den im wesentlichen klassischen Entwurf durchzieht: »Dies ist ein faszinierendes Bauwerk, und zwar aufgrund seiner großen Schönheit, wenn auch einer Schönheit, bei der Unordnung durchschimmert – über und unter der ruhigen Oberfläche. Gerade wegen der Konfusion wird ihr wahres Wesen offenbart. In starkem Kontrast zur Farbe Weiß (Zahl und Vernunft) entwickeln sich Formen, die negativ und bedrohlich wirken: ein dunkles, anthropomorphes Gebilde am Treppenaufgang; ein sich langsam entrollendes Meeresgeschöpf, das sich jeden Augenblick in seine Schneckenschale zurückziehen und somit den Zugang zum Inneren versperren könnte; eine zusammenbrechende Konstruktion, die in einem bestimmten Moment ihres Falls erstarrt ist; die unausweichliche Gegenwart der zwei hoch aufragenden Schlote im Hintergrund: Fabrikschornsteine, schwarzen Rauch ausstoßend, den wir bald einatmen müssen. Die bizarren, knotigen Äste einer Korkeiche, die sich in den Himmel recken.«[6]

Man hat vermutet, Siza habe sein Gebäude in Setúbal sorgfältig um eben diesen Baum herum angelegt, er selbst beschreibt den tatsächlichen Entwurfsprozeß allerdings genauer: »Auf dem Baugelände standen sehr viele Bäume, wir mußten jedoch einige fällen, die dem Bau im Wege standen. Ich gab die Anweisung, so viele Bäume wie möglich zu retten. Als die Fällarbeiten beendet waren, merkte ich erst, daß dieser Baum exakt im Zentrum stehengeblieben war. Für mich war das wie ein Wunder. Wahrscheinlich hätte ich einen neuen Baum genau an dieser Stelle gepflanzt, wenn der alte nicht gewesen wäre. Alle denken, ich hätte das Gebäude extra so geplant, daß der Baum im Zentrum erhalten blieb. Nein, ich hatte einfach Glück, daß er dort stand.«[7]

Die Frage nach den Einflüssen auf den Architekturstil Álvaro Sizas wird häufig gestellt. Im Fall des Ausbildungsinstitutes für Lehrer in Setúbal werden häufig Namen wie Adolf Loos oder Luis Barragán genannt. Ein anderes Universitätsgebäude von Siza legt eine noch deutlichere Referenz nahe: Die Bibliothek der Universität Aveiro (1988–95) ist eines seiner vollkommensten und gelungensten Werke. Das Gebäude steht im Zentrum eines modernen Universitätskomplexes und folgt mit seinen Ziegelsteinfassaden und Kalksteindetails den Stilvorgaben für alle Bauten der Universität. Siza hat

> Bonjour Tristesse Apartment Building, Schlesisches Tor, Kreuzberg, Berlin, Germany, 1980–84

began. Oscar Niemeyer and Le Corbusier were also very influential. I am sure that my work has been influenced by that of Alvar Aalto, as it has been by hundreds of other architects. If you fix one influence, you are lost. To learn architecture is to know the work of many different designers."[8]

From Porto to Aveiro and Setúbal, Siza's university buildings, recently joined by his Rectory for the University of Alicante, do exhibit a certain complexity that is not entirely typical of the Modern Movement. These are not placid buildings, clearly situated in the tradition of modern classicism, but somehow of another breed, daring to introduce an element of uneasiness. It would seem to be no accident that the stairway that floods incongruously into the entrance of the Carlos Ramos Pavilion at the Faculty of Architecture in Porto has been compared to that in Michelangelo's Laurentian Library (Florence, Italy, 1524–26) which announced the arrival of Mannerism. And yet all of these buildings do offer convivial work and study spaces. They do not turn their backs on their surroundings in the style of much true Modernism; rather they impose their unexpected presence on an environment to which they duly pay their respect, be it in the case of the lone tree in the central courtyard in Setúbal, or in the windows opening out onto the marshlands in Aveiro, or the complex relationships of the Faculty of Architecture to its urban and natural setting.

CAPITAL AMBITIONS

The status of Álvaro Siza within Portugal is clearly indicated by three recent projects in his country's capital, Lisbon. His work on a very large subway station, with one exit in the city's Chiado neighborhood, might be considered symbolic of the renaissance of an area that was ravaged by fires in August of 1988. With responsibility for the overall planning of the reconstruction effort, Siza has restored two neighboring structures, the Camara Chaves (1991–96) and Castro & Melo buildings (1991–94), with several

d'une université moderne, le bâtiment a adopté un revêtement en brique et des parements en pierre calcaire spécifiés par le code de construction de l'institution. Presque chaque détail, des rampes des escaliers aux comptoirs en porte-à-faux et à chaque luminaire, a été conçu par l'architecte lui-même. Les fenêtres offrent des vues soigneusement cadrées sur les terrains marécageux avoisinants, rappelant certaines réalisations antérieures dont le restaurant Boa Nova, mais également des créations plus récentes comme l'église de Marco. Sur la façade ouest, qui donne sur les marais, un mur de brique ondulé rappelle la maison de la culture d'Alvar Aalto (Helsinki, Finlande, 1952–58), tandis que l'espace intérieur pourrait évoquer la salle à manger-séjour de Baker House, une résidence pour étudiants du M.I.T. (Cambridge, Massachusetts, 1946–49), ou la Mount Angel Abbey Library (St. Benedict, Oregon, 1964–70) du même architecte. Lorsqu'on l'interroge aujourd'hui sur l'influence d'Aalto dans son travail, Siza répond: «Dans l'Italie, l'Espagne et le Portugal des années 50, Aalto a exercé une grande influence, et ce pour deux raisons. Dans l'ambiance de l'architecture de l'après-guerre, la reconstruction était menée de façon industrielle en France, en Allemagne et aux Pays-Bas. Les pays périphériques, comme le Portugal n'étaient pas aussi industrialisés. Au Portugal et en Espagne, la situation présentait certains points communs avec celle de la Finlande. Dans ce pays, il était difficile de trouver du ciment, mais les artisans qui savaient travailler le bois étaient disponibles. Alvar Aalto devint ainsi une très importante référence. Il s'est rendu à plusieurs reprises en Espagne, en Afrique du Nord, en Grèce et un peu au Portugal. Il a rapporté beaucoup d'éléments de l'architecture de ces pays en Finlande. Se sont alors développés des relations et des échanges qui ont exercé un impact sur mon école lorsque j'ai débuté. Oscar Niemeyer et Le Corbusier ont également été très influents. Je suis certain que mon œuvre a été influencée par celle d'Aalto, mais aussi par des centaines d'autres architectes. Si vous isolez une influence, vous êtes perdu.

nahezu sämtliche Details – von Treppenhandläufen bis zu den frei vorkragenden Theken und jeder Leuchte im Gebäude – selbst entworfen. Die Fenster bieten mit Bedacht gerahmte Ausblicke auf die Marschlandschaft und erinnern an frühe Bauten von Siza wie das Restaurant Boa Nova, aber auch an jüngere Entwürfe wie etwa seine Kirche in Marco. Die geschwungene Westfassade (zum Marschland hin) erinnert stark an Alvar Aaltos Kulturhaus (Helsinki, Finnland, 1952–58), während die Innenräume Anklänge an Aaltos Mensa und Aufenthaltsraum im Studentenwohnheim Baker House auf dem Campus des Massachusetts Institute of Technology (Cambridge, Massachusetts, 1946–49) bieten, oder an Aaltos Mount Angel Abbey Library (St. Benedict, Oregon, 1964–70).

Fragt man Siza heute nach dem Einfluß von Aaltos Architektur auf seine eigene, erklärt er: »In den 50ern hat Aalto in Italien, Spanien und Portugal großen Einfluß ausgeübt. Dafür gibt es zwei Gründe: Im Bauwesen der Nachkriegszeit wurde der Wiederaufbau in Frankreich, Deutschland und den Niederlanden sozusagen industriell betrieben. Die Randländer Europas waren nicht so hoch industrialisiert und die Situation in Portugal oder Spanien daher in vielen Punkten ähnlich wie die in Finnland. In Finnland war Zement schwer zu bekommen, es gab jedoch Handwerker, die mit Holz arbeiten konnten. Alvar Aalto wurde ein sehr wichtiges Vorbild. Er reiste mehrfach nach Spanien, Nordafrika und Griechenland und besuchte auch Portugal. Viele Elemente, die er in diesen Ländern sah, nahm er mit zurück nach Finnland. Einige dieser Bezüge und Einflüsse wirkten sich auch auf meinen Architekturstil aus, als ich am Anfang meiner Laufbahn stand. Oscar Niemeyer und Le Corbusier haben mich ebenfalls stark beeinflußt. Ich bin sicher, daß meine Arbeit durch das Werk von Aalto genauso beeinflußt wurde wie durch das 100 anderer Architekten. Wenn man sich nur auf eine Quelle fixiert, ist man verloren. Den Beruf des Architekten erlernen heißt, das Werk vieler Architekten studieren.«[8]

Von Porto bis Aveiro und Setúbal legen Sizas Universitätsgebäude – vor kurzem ergänzt durch sein Dekanat der Universität Alicante – eine gewisse Vielgestaltigkeit an den Tag, die für die Moderne untypisch ist. Es sind keine ruhigen, reduzierten Bauten, die man der klassischen Moderne eindeutig zuordnen könnte, sondern sie haben sozusagen einen anderen architektonischen »Stammbaum«, weil der Architekt es gewagt hat, ein unruhiges Element in den Entwurf einzuführen. Nicht zufällig wird die Treppe, die in buchstäblich unangemessener Weise in den Eingang des Carlos-Ramos-Pavillons (Architekturfakultät) der Universität Porto »hineinfließt«, mit Michelangelos Treppe der Biblioteca Laurenziana (Florenz, Italien, 1524–26) verglichen, die den Beginn des Manierismus markiert. Und dennoch bieten alle Universitätsgebäude von Siza einladende Arbeits- und Unterrichtsräume. Anders als viele typische Gebäude der klassischen Moderne zeigen sie ihrer Umgebung nicht »die kalte Schulter«, sondern behaupten sich mit ihrer unerwarteten Präsenz in einem Kontext, dem sie die ihm zustehende Referenz erweisen – zum Beispiel mit dem Baum im zentralen Innenhof in Setúbal, mit den Fenstern in Aveiro, die den Blick auf das Schwemmland öffnen,

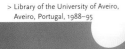
> Library of the University of Aveiro, Aveiro, Portugal, 1988–95

more to come. From the outside neither of these buildings shows obvious signs of Siza's style, because it was decided to retain the original facades. As Siza says, "I was asked to use the surviving facades. It was a decision of the politicians, but I accepted, because it was also my opinion. Lisbon's center, the Baixa, can be seen as a gigantic prefabricated building. Because eighteen buildings were destroyed, some wanted to add modern buildings to the Chiado, but modernity is already very present in Lisbon. There was no need to make a statement about modernity in the Chiado. Fundamentally, the same is never the same. Modern comfort and building capacities have been added to these buildings. It was never possible to really recreate the spaces that existed before the fire. The buildings had all been modified over the past two centuries, and no longer corresponded to their original plans. The eclecticism that resulted from the spontaneous workings of time could not be recreated, but something of this remained in the facades."[9]

Henrique Chaves, the promoter responsible for the Camara Chaves project, proudly shows his own apartment, where the subtle and very complete intervention of Siza becomes apparent. Although the spaces of this rooftop apartment are inspired by what existed before, the same, as the architect says, is never the same. This is particularly true because in these flowing, modern spaces almost every detail of the furnishings and fixtures has been designed by Siza.

By far the most visible of Siza's Lisbon buildings, the Portuguese Pavilion, located at the heart of the Expo '98 fairgrounds, is to be the future home of the country's Council of Ministers. With its great curving veil of concrete coupled with a fundamental austerity, it takes on an almost iconic force. Although he asked Eduardo Souto de Moura to design interior spaces related to the multimedia and art presentations in the pavilion, Siza has elsewhere carried through the project down to the last details. This is particularly visible in the restaurant, or in the VIP areas on the

Apprendre l'architecture, c'est connaître le travail de nombreux, de très nombreux créateurs.»[8]

De Porto à Aveiro et à Setúbal, les bâtiments universitaires de Siza – auxquels vient s'ajouter son récent rectorat pour l'Université d'Alicante – affichent une certaine complexité qui n'est pas entièrement caractéristique du mouvement moderne. Loin d'être des constructions placides, clairement situées dans les limites de la tradition du classicisme moderne, elles appartiennent à une sorte d'autre race, qui ose introduire un élément troublant. Ce n'est pas par accident que l'escalier qui fait une irruption incongrue dans l'entrée du pavillon Carlos Ramos de la faculté d'architecture de Porto a été comparé à celui de Michel-Ange dans la bibliothèque laurentienne (Florence, Italie, 1524–26), qui annonce l'arrivée du maniérisme. Et cependant, tous ces bâtiments offrent des espaces de travail et d'étude conviviaux. Il ne tournent pas le dos à leur environnement comme tant de réalisations authentiquement modernes, mais lui imposent plutôt leur présence inattendue et lui rendent dûment hommage, que ce soit dans le cas de l'arbre solitaire de la cour centrale de Setúbal, ou dans les ouvertures sur les marais d'Aveiro, ou encore dans les relations complexes entre la faculté d'architecture et son cadre urbain et naturel.

AMBITIONS CAPITALES

Le statut d'Álvaro Siza au Portugal apparaît en pleine lumière dans trois projets récents conçus pour Lisbonne. Son travail sur une très grande station de métro, qui possède une sortie sur le quartier de Chiado, peut être considéré comme symbolique de la renaissance de cette zone ravagée par des incendies en août 1988. Responsable de la totalité de la planification, Siza n'a restauré pour l'instant que deux immeubles voisins, la Camara Chaves (1991–96) et les bâtiments Castro & Melo (1991–94), mais d'autres suivront. De l'extérieur, aucune de ces constructions n'exprime le style de l'architecte puisqu'il a été décidé de

oder mit den vielfältigen Beziehungen des Architekturfakultätsgebäudes zu seiner städtischen und landschaftlichen Umgebung.

HAUPTSTADTAMBITIONEN

Drei neuere Projekte in Lissabon geben deutliche Hinweise auf Sizas Rang in Portugal. Sein Bau einer sehr großen U-Bahnstation mit einem ihrer Ausgänge im Bereich des Stadtteils Chiado könnte als Symbol für den Wiederaufbau des im August 1988 durch einen Brand zerstörten Innenstadtareals gelten. Siza hatte die Verantwortung für die Gesamtplanung des Aufbaus und restaurierte bzw. rekonstruierte zwei benachbarte Bauten, die Gebäude der Firmen Camara Chaves (1991–96) und Castro & Melo (1991–94). Weitere sollen folgen. Von außen zeigen beide keine deutlichen Zeichen von Sizas Baustil, da die Originalfassaden beibehalten wurden. »Ich wurde gebeten,« so Siza, »die stehengebliebenen Außenmauern zu erhalten. Das war eine baupolitische Entscheidung, die ich aber voll akzeptierte, da sie meiner eigenen Auffassung entsprach. Das heutige Zentrum von Lissabon, die Baixa, ist praktisch ein einziges gigantisches, vorfabriziertes Bauwerk. Da 18 Gebäude völlig zerstört waren, wollten einige [Architekten] im Chiado-Bezirk neue und moderne anstelle der historischen Häuser bauen. Die moderne Architektur ist jedoch in Lissabon bereits stark vertreten, und es bestand keine Notwendigkeit, hier eine Aussage zur modernen Architektur zu machen. Grundsätzlich gilt ja, daß das gleiche nie dasselbe ist. Beim Wiederaufbau wurden moderner Komfort und neue Baumöglichkeiten realisiert. Es war bei keiner Rekonstruktion möglich, exakt die gleichen Räume wie vor dem Brand wiederherzustellen. Die Gebäude waren alle im Laufe der vergangenen zwei Jahrhunderte umgebaut worden und entsprachen längst nicht mehr den ursprünglichen Bauplänen. Der aus diesen spontanen Eingriffen resultierende ›Eklektizismus‹ konnte nicht wieder erzielt werden, dennoch ist etwas davon in den Fassaden zurückgeblieben.«[9]

Henrique Chaves, der für das Camara Chaves-Projekt verantwortliche Bauherr, zeigt stolz seine eigene Wohnung, in der die subtilen und umfassenden Eingriffe Álvaro Sizas deutlich werden. Obwohl die Gestaltung dieser Dachetage von der zuvor bestehenden historischen Innenarchitektur abgeleitet ist, ist sie – wie der Architekt betont hat – die gleiche und doch nicht dieselbe geblieben. Hier gilt dies in ganz besonderer Weise, da Siza fast jedes Detail der Innenausstattung und -einrichtung dieser fließenden modernen Innenräume entworfen hat.

Der Portugiesische Pavillon im Herzen des Expo-Geländes von 1998 ist das buchstäblich hervorstechendste Werk Sizas in Lissabon und das zukünftige Domizil des Ministerrats der Regierung. Mit seiner riesigen geschwungenen Sichtbetonwand im Verbund mit grundlegender Schlichtheit ist das Gebäude von fast ikonischer Kraft. Siza beauftragte zwar Eduardo Souto de Moura mit dem Entwurf der Innenausstattung in den Bereichen der Multi-Media- und Kunstausstellung des Expo-Pavillons,

upper level, where every piece of furniture, and even some of the tableware, is designed by him. Figures freely drawn by Siza in red adorn the dining area walls. An interesting detail of this pervasive presence is that the architect's touch remains light, unobtrusive. Nowhere is his signature, or even his name, in evidence.

As for the unusual configuration of the Portuguese Pavilion, Siza's own words best describe how it came about: "I was asked to provide 3,500 square meters of covered space for ceremonies, receptions for heads of state and so forth. I realized that this area should not have pillars. I tried other solutions. I looked at Asplund's buildings, or Niemeyer's covered spaces. I began working with very good engineers, a group in Lisbon and Ove Arup, and at first I imagined a roof that would curve up, but that would have made the structure quite high. As the Expo site was designed, the relationship between buildings was not really considered. The plan was not strong enough, and everyone began to work at the same time. The site was in an axial location vis-à-vis the dock. I asked that a large space be left open in front of the building, but I noticed that many of the neighboring buildings were starting to look very big, or at least to have big 'hair-do's.' So I thought that my building should be horizontal, which led me to try the idea of a curve in the opposite direction for the covering of the open space. The engineers liked the idea and said they could do it. We studied how to finish the ends with the steel cables. We decided to leave an opening so that light can enter. It developed step by step. Within the building, I needed great flexibility, because they could not tell me what it would be used for. I decided to modulate the structure and the windows in such a way that different programs could be accommodated, for example by dividing the spaces. I made a central patio to bring light into the center. It became a very simple building, which reacts to the sweeping curve of the other part of the structure. Some people said to me that the curve resembles the sail of a boat. I don't reject that idea, but it was not part of the design process."[10]

conserver les façades anciennes. Comme le déclare Siza: «On m'a demandé d'utiliser les façades subsistantes. Ce fut une décision des hommes politiques, que j'ai acceptée parce que c'était également mon opinion. Le centre de Lisbonne, la Baixa, peut être considéré comme un immense bâtiment préfabriqué. Comme 18 immeubles avaient été détruits, certains voulaient reconstruire à neuf, mais la modernité est déjà très présente à Lisbonne. Il n'y avait aucune raison de prendre un parti pris de modernité dans le Chiado. Fondamentalement, la même chose n'est jamais la même. Ces immeubles ont été dotés du confort moderne et de nouvelles surfaces. Il n'a jamais été possible de réellement recréer les espaces qui existaient avant l'incendie. Tous ces immeubles avaient été modifiés au cours des deux derniers siècles et ne correspondaient plus à leurs plans d'origine. L'éclectisme né du travail spontané du temps ne pouvait être recréé, mais quelque chose en est resté dans les façades.»[9]

Henrique Chaves, le promoteur responsable du projet Camara Chaves, est fier de présenter sa demeure dans laquelle les interventions à la fois subtiles et en profondeur de Siza apparaissent nettement. Bien que les espaces de cet appartement situé au dernier étage de l'immeuble s'inspirent de ce qui existait auparavant, «le même n'est jamais le même», comme aime à dire Siza. C'est particulièrement vrai dans ces espaces modernes et fluides, dont presque chaque détail du mobilier et des équipements a été dessiné par l'architecte.

La plus «visible» des réalisations de Siza à Lisbonne, le Pavillon du Portugal de l'Expo '98, devrait abriter bientôt le Conseil des Ministres du pays. Son immense voile de béton incurvé, et son austérité fondamentale lui confèrent d'ores et déjà une présence iconique. Bien qu'il ait demandé à Eduardo Souto de Moura de dessiner les espaces intérieurs destinés aux expositions artistiques et multimédias du pavillon, partout ailleurs, Siza a pris en charge le projet, jusque dans ses moindres détails. C'est particulièrement visible dans le restaurant et les salons VIP du niveau supérieur

ansonsten war er aber selbst verantwortlich für die gesamte Innenarchitektur – bis hin zum kleinsten Detail. Dies ist besonders augenfällig im Restaurant oder in den VIP-Bereichen im Obergeschoß, für die er jedes Möbelstück und sogar einen Teil des Geschirrs entwarf. Figürliche Handzeichnungen in rot von Álvaro Siza zieren die Wände des Restaurantbereichs. Das Interessante an der gestalterischen Allgegenwärtigkeit des Architekten ist, daß er mit leichter Hand und unauffällig gewirkt hat. Nirgendwo taucht seine »Signatur« oder gar sein Name auf.

Sizas eigene Worte sind am besten geeignet, die ungewöhnliche Gestalt des portugiesischen Pavillons zu erklären: »Ich sollte 3500 Quadratmeter überdachten Raum für offizielle Anlässe, z.B. Staatsempfänge, schaffen. Mir war klar, daß dieser Raum nicht von Säulen unterbrochen werden durfte. Ich suchte nach anderen Lösungen, schaute mir etwa Gunnar Asplunds Bauwerke an oder Oscar Niemeyers Räume mit großen Spannweiten. Ich zog sehr gute Bauingenieure hinzu, ein Büro in Lissabon und Ove Arup & Partners, und konzipierte als erstes ein aufwärts schwingendes Dach, wodurch das Gebäude recht hoch geworden wäre. Bei der Planung der Expo-Anlage spielte das Verhältnis der einzelnen Bauten zueinander eigentlich keine Rolle. Der Gesamtplan war nicht dominant genug, und alle begannen gleichzeitig mit der Arbeit. Das Gelände liegt axial zur gegenüberliegenden Hafenanlage. Ich beantragte einen großen Freiplatz vor meinem Pavillon, bemerkte dann jedoch, daß viele benachbarte Pavillons als hoch aufragende Gebäude geplant waren oder zumindest ›Turmfrisuren‹ bekommen sollten. Deshalb beschloß ich, mein Gebäude in der Horizontale anzulegen, und mir kam die Idee, ein konkav gewölbtes Dach zur Überdachung des offenen Raums vorzusehen. Den Ingenieuren gefiel diese Idee und sie sagten, daß sie sie umsetzen könnten. Wir untersuchten Möglichkeiten, die Enden mit Stahlseilen zu fixieren. Wir entschieden uns, zwecks Lichteinfall eine Öffnung zu lassen. Alles entwickelte sich Schritt für Schritt. Im Innern des Gebäudes brauchte ich große Flexibilität, denn die Auftraggeber konnten mir nicht sagen, wie es schließlich genutzt werden würde. Ich beschloß, die Struktur und die Fenstergliederung so aufzuteilen, daß der Bau unterschiedlichen Nutzungen zugeführt werden konnte, zum Beispiel mittels Raumteilungen. Ich schuf einen zentralen Patio, um Licht ins Gebäudeinnere zu bringen. Schließlich entstand ein sehr schlichter Bau, der im Dialog mit dem großen Schwung der Außenkonstruktion steht. Einige Leute sagten mir, diese erinnere sie an Bootssegel. Ich widerspreche dem zwar nicht, aber bei der Entwurfsarbeit hat diese Vorstellung keine Rolle gespielt.«[10]

ZWEI MUSEEN

Nach Aussagen von Sizas Mitarbeitern ist das Galicische Museum für Zeitgenössische Kunst im spanischen Santiago de Compostela (1988–93) eines der Bauprojekte, das den Architekten in den letzten Jahren am intensivsten beschäftigt hat. Es steht auf dem Gelände eines früheren Obstgartens des

> Portuguese Pavilion, Expo '98
Lisbon, Portugal, 1995–98

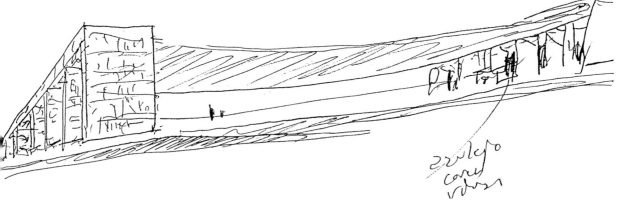

TWO MUSEUMS

According to his collaborators, one of the projects that has most interested and absorbed Álvaro Siza in recent years is his Galician Center for Contemporary Art (Santiago de Compostela, Spain, 1988–93). Situated on a triangular lot within the boundaries of the former orchard of the 17th century Convent of Santo Domingo de Bonaval, and bounded by the Valle-Inclán square, the site of the Galician Center for Contemporary Art is intimately related to a larger area including the Convent of San Roque, the Camino Gateway, and the houses situated between das Rodas Street and Valle-Inclán Street. Emerging from the hillside, the granite facades of the museum do somehow achieve the delicate balance and harmony between past and present sought by the architect.

"I have the pretension," he says, "to say that it refers to the entire history of the city and not only to its own time. This results not from a removal of historical references, but from an attempt at creating a synthesis. The facades of the museum," continues the architect, "are monumental because they have almost no windows. Because of their lack of detail, they can achieve a strength that is equal to that of the church or the convent. Within, the museum does not suggest an itinerary to the visitor, but rather a series of alternatives. One of our problems with this project was that at the beginning, there was neither a collection nor a curator. Our only choice was to offer a flexible system, permitting various different types of use."[11] Part of this flexibility was achieved through the use of a plan made up of two overlapping L-shaped volumes. Both on the outside, and within, an emphasis has been placed on a purity of line. The white interiors, with Greek marble flooring in the public areas, are rendered all the more pure through a suspended ceiling, concealing security systems and lighting sources.

In the case of this project, the architect was also responsible for the Santo Domingo de Bonaval Garden (1990–94). This fact may highlight Siza's interest in landscape, at least on those occasions où chaque meuble et même certaines pièces de vaisselle ont été dessinés par lui. Des figures en rouge, d'un trait très libre, œuvres de l'architecte, ornent les murs de la salle à manger. Détail significatif dans cette omniprésence: l'intervention de Siza reste légère et discrète. Nulle part sa signature ou même son nom n'apparaissent en évidence.

«On m'a demandé de fournir 3500 m² d'espaces couverts pour les cérémonies, les réceptions de chefs d'État et autres manifestations. Il m'a semblé que ce lieu ne devait pas avoir de piliers. J'ai essayé d'autres solutions. J'ai regardé du côté des réalisations d'Asplund ou des espaces couverts de Niemeyer. J'ai commencé à travailler avec de très bons ingénieurs – une agence de Lisbonne et Ove Arup & Partners – et j'ai débuté par un toit à courbe convexe, mais qui aurait entraîné une construction assez haute. Lors de la conception urbanistique de l'Expo, la relation entre les diverses constructions n'a pas été réellement prise en considération. Le plan n'était pas assez fort, et tout le monde a commencé à travailler en même temps. Le site est axé par rapport au dock. J'ai demandé qu'un grand espace soit laissé dégagé devant le bâtiment, mais j'ai remarqué qu'un grand nombre des constructions voisines commençaient à prendre beaucoup d'importance, ou du moins à se pousser du col; j'ai ainsi pensé que ma construction devait rester horizontale, ce qui m'a conduit à tenter une courbe en sens opposé pour couvrir l'espace ouvert. Les ingénieurs ont aimé cette idée et m'ont assuré que c'était possible. Nous avons particulièrement étudié les extrémités et l'attache des câbles d'acier, et décidé de laisser une ouverture afin que la lumière puisse pénétrer. Le projet s'est développé étape par étape. Pour l'intérieur, j'avais besoin de beaucoup de souplesse, car on n'était pas capable de me dire à l'époque ce que l'on allait y mettre. J'ai décidé de moduler la structure et les fenêtres de façon à ce que différents types de programmes puissent y trouver place, en divisant les espaces, par exemple. J'ai dessiné un patio central, pour faire pénétrer la lumière dans cette partie. C'est

Klosters Santo Domingo de Bonaval aus dem 17. Jahrhundert und wird vom Valle-Inclán-Platz begrenzt. Der Baugrund des Museums ist Teil eines größeren Stadtareals, das auch das Kloster San Roque, das Camino-Tor und die Häuser zwischen den Straßen Rua Rodas und Rua Valle-Inclán umfaßt. Es ist dem Architekten gelungen, mit den Granitfassaden des Museumsbaus die angestrebte Ausgewogenheit von Historie und Moderne herzustellen. »Ich maße mir an zu behaupten«, so Álvaro Siza, »daß das Gebäude sich auf die gesamte Stadtgeschichte bezieht und nicht nur auf seine eigene Zeit. Das resultiert nicht aus dem Entfernen historischer Bezüge, sondern aus dem Versuch einer Synthese. Die Fassaden sind monumental, weil sie fast keine Fensteröffnungen haben. Aufgrund ihres Detailmangels erreichen sie eine der Kirche oder dem Klosterbau entsprechende Ausdruckskraft. Die Innengliederung schreibt dem Besucher keinen bestimmten Weg durch das Museum vor, sondern bietet ihm eine Reihe von Möglichkeiten an. Eines unserer Probleme mit dem Entwurf bestand darin, daß es am Anfang weder eine Sammlung noch einen Kurator gab. Die einzig mögliche Lösung war daher eine flexible Gliederung, die unterschiedliche Nutzungen erlaubt.«[11] Zum Teil wurde diese Flexibilität erreicht durch einen Grundriß, der aus zwei sich überschneidenden L-Formen besteht. Innen wie außen liegt der Schwerpunkt der Gestaltung auf einer klaren Linienführung. Die weißen Innenräume mit Fußböden aus griechischem Marmor in den Publikumsbereichen werden noch klarer und makelloser durch abgehängte Decken, hinter denen Sicherheitssysteme und Beleuchtungskörper verborgen sind.

Zu diesem Bauauftrag gehörte auch die Planung des Santo Domingo de Bonaval-Parks (1990–94), ein gutes Beispiel für Sizas Interesse an Landschaftsgestaltung, zumindest in Fällen, in denen sich ihm die Gelegenheit bietet, seinen Gestaltungswillen auch auf die Umgebung seiner Bauten auszudehnen. Sizas Betonwände oder unbehauenen Natursteinmauern sind wichtige, augenfällige Elemente bei Bauwerken wie dem Meeresschwimmbad in Leça da Palmeira, der Architekturfakultät der Universität Porto oder dem Haus Vieira de Castro in Famalicão. Zum Galicischen Museum für Zeitgenössische Kunst sagt Siza: »Ich kann es nicht genau erklären, bin aber fest davon überzeugt – weil ich Santiago viele Male besucht habe –, daß sich der Neubau auf sehr natürliche Weise in diese Stadtlandschaft einpaßt.« Das Wort »Landschaft« scheint hier besonders bezeichnend zu sein – wie überhaupt in Sizas gesamtem Schaffen.

Eines von Álvaro Sizas jüngsten Projekten wird zweifellos mehrere Gemeinsamkeiten mit dem Galicischen Museum für Zeitgenössische Kunst aufweisen. Es handelt sich um den Neubau der Serralves-Stiftung in Porto in der Quinta de Serralves, einem der größten Parkareale der Stadt. Die Serralves-Stiftung wurde gemeinschaftlich von der portugiesischen Regierung und 50 Partnern der Privatwirtschaft gegründet und widmet sich einem ehrgeizigen Ausstellungsprogramm für Gegenwartskunst, besitzt aber derzeit noch keine bedeutende Sammlung. Auf die Frage, wie er mit

where the natural or urban setting offers him an opportunity to express himself outside of the main structure. His concrete or rusticated stone walls appear as prominent features in such projects as the Leça Swimming Pool, the Faculty of Architecture in Porto, or the Vieira de Castro House. Siza says of the Galician Center, "I can't say exactly why, but I am convinced, because I have visited Santiago intensively, that the building seems very natural in this urban landscape." The word "landscape" seems particularly significant here, as it has been throughout Siza's career.

One of Álvaro Siza's most recent projects will undoubtedly have several points in common with the Galician Center. His new structure for the Serralves Foundation in Porto is located in the Quinta de Serralves, one of the largest park areas in the city. Created through a unique partnership between the Portuguese government and fifty private sector partners, the Serralves Foundation is committed to an ambitious program of contemporary art exhibitions, but does not, at least for the time being, have a significant collection. When asked how he deals with programs that are necessarily vague, as was the case in Santiago, and now for Serralves, Siza replies with typical humor. "As far as the lack of a solid program is concerned, I use the Japanese way with judo. If you cannot fight something, you accept it. A lack of definition requires a flexible design. In contemporary art museums the question is more and more one of organizing temporary exhibitions. Even in museums with very good permanent collections of contemporary art, they change the presentations regularly – they even use the collections to organize temporary exhibitions. The problem in those museums is not to create a scenario with special pieces, but to create spaces that allow different uses – flexibility, and a certain neutrality. Not the neutrality that some curators want, which is non-architecture or a void. A museum, I think must have its own character and be related to the milieu where it is. It also must be able to receive

devenu un bâtiment très simple, qui réagit au mouvement en courbe de l'autre partie de la structure. Certains m'ont dit que cette courbe faisait penser à une voile de bateau. Je ne rejette pas cette idée, mais elle n'a joué aucun rôle dans la conception de ce projet.»[10]

DEUX MUSÉES

Selon ses collaborateurs, l'un des projets qui a le plus intéressé et absorbé Álvaro Siza au cours de ces dernières années est le Centre d'Art Contemporain de Galice (Saint-Jacques de Compostelle, Espagne, 1988–93). Situé à l'intérieur de l'ancien verger du couvent de Santo Domingo de Bonaval (XVIIe siècle), et donnant sur la place de Valle-Inclán, le site de cet équipement culturel est intimement lié à un secteur historique plus vaste qui comprend le couvent de San Roque, la porte du Camino et les maisons situées entre la rue Rodas et la rue Valle-Inclán. Émergeant du flanc de la colline, les façades de granit du musée parviennent d'une certaine façon à un délicat équilibre entre le passé et le présent, effet recherché par l'architecte. «J'ai la prétention», dit-il, «d'affirmer que [ce centre] se réfère à l'histoire entière de la ville et non seulement à son époque.» Ceci vient non de la suppression de références historiques, mais de la tentative d'en créer une synthèse. «Les façades du musée sont monumentales parce qu'elles ne possèdent presque pas de fenêtres. Du fait de leur manque de détail, elle atteignent une force égale à celle de l'église ou du couvent. À l'intérieur, le musée ne suggère pas d'itinéraire à son visiteur, mais plutôt une série d'alternatives. L'un de nos problèmes pour ce projet a été qu'au départ, il n'y avait ni collection ni conservateur. Notre seule possibilité était de prévoir un système souple qui permette différents types d'usages.»[11]
Une partie de cette flexibilité a été obtenue grâce à un plan composé de deux volumes en «L» se chevauchant. À l'intérieur comme à l'extérieur, l'accent a été mis sur la pureté des lignes. Les intérieurs blancs, à sols en marbre grec dans les parties

almost everything."[12] Set at a certain distance from the existing foundation building, an art deco house built in the 1930s for the Count of Vizela, the new structure includes 3 hectares of landscaping work, which will "help graft the new construction into the surroundings." Within the museum, several very large, high exhibition galleries have ceilings including a slab of concrete, which appears to hover just below the roof. This device permits modulated daylight to be brought onto the exhibition surfaces, and also allows the technical conduits, including artificial lighting, to be hidden from view. This system was also used in the Galician Center by Siza, giving it not only excellent natural and artificial lighting, but also an apparent simplicity that underscores the entire architectural design.

The architect offers the following "morphological" description of the Serralves Foundation: "There is a main body from which two asymmetrical wings are generated southward, creating a courtyard between them, and an L-shaped volume set to the north, creating between itself and the center body another courtyard, in the public access area of the building." Built with an obviously ample budget, the Serralves Foundation also has the advantage of being set in a truly beautiful park, a fact that the architect recalls with a number of strategically located windows, which frame carefully constructed views of the environment.

A CHURCH AND A HOUSE
Two buildings completed recently by Álvaro Siza offer a concentrated view of his originality and of the power of his work. The first of these is the Santa Maria Church (Marco de Canavezes, 1990–96), located a half-hour drive north of Porto. Indeed, the church itself had not been fully completed in June of 1998, with important details such as the 10 meter high bronze doors still missing; above all, the Parish Center, planned by the architect as part of an overall complex forming a small urban square, had not yet been built. And yet it is possible to understand the importance

publiques, sont encore davantage épurés par un plafond suspendu qui dissimule les systèmes de sécurité et d'éclairage. Dans le cadre de ce projet, l'architecte a également été chargé du jardin de Santo Domingo de Bonaval (1990–94), ce qui est révélateur de l'intérêt qu'il porte au paysage, du moins dans les cas où le cadre naturel ou urbain lui offre l'opportunité de s'exprimer hors de la construction elle-même. Ses murs de béton ou de pierre rustiquée sont des caractéristiques frappantes de projets comme la piscine de Leça da Palmeira, la faculté d'architecture de Porto ou la maison Vieira de Castro de Famalicão. Siza ajoute, en parlant de ce centre galicien: «Je ne peux dire exactement pourquoi, mais je suis convaincu, parce que j'ai visité Saint-Jacques de façon approfondie, que le bâtiment semble tout à fait naturel dans ce paysage urbain.» Le mot de «paysage» semble particulièrement significatif ici, comme dans toute l'œuvre de l'architecte.

L'un des plus récents projets d'Álvaro Siza possède sans aucun doute plusieurs points communs avec le centre de Galice. Le nouveau bâtiment de la Fondation Serralves à Porto se trouve dans la Quinta de Serralves, l'un des plus vastes parcs de la ville. Créé grâce à un partenariat original entre le gouvernement portugais et cinquante représentants du secteur privé, la Fondation s'est donné pour objectif un ambitieux programme d'expositions d'art contemporain, sans posséder, du moins pour l'instant, de collection significative. Lorsqu'on le questionne sur sa manière de travailler face à des programmes nécessairement vagues, comme à Saint-Jacques et pour Serralves, Siza réplique avec son humour habituel: «Pour ce qui est du manque de programme, je fais appel à la technique des judokas japonais. Si vous ne pouvez combattre quelque chose, efforcez-vous de l'accepter. Un manque de définition programmatique exige une conception souple. Dans les musées d'art contemporain, le problème est de plus en plus celui de l'organisation d'expositions temporaires. Même dans les musées qui possèdent de bonnes

< Santa Maria Church, Marco de Canavezes, Portugal, 1990–96

> Santa Maria Church, Marco de Canavezes, Portugal, 1990–96

collections permanentes, la présentation change périodiquement, et ils organisent des manifestations temporaires à partir de leurs collections. Le problème des musées n'est pas de créer un scénario pour des œuvres spécifiques, mais des espaces qui permettent différents usages: il faut de la souplesse et une certaine neutralité. Mais pas la neutralité souhaitée par certains conservateurs, qui est une non-architecture ou un vide. Je crois qu'un musée doit posséder son caractère propre et entretenir des liens avec le milieu qui est le sien. Il doit être également capable d'accueillir presque n'importe quoi.»[12]

Implantée à une certaine distance du bâtiment de la Fondation – une maison de style Art Déco construite dans les années 30 pour le comte de Vizela – la nouvelle structure s'élève au milieu de 3 hectares de terrain paysager qui «aideront à ancrer la nouvelle construction dans son environnement». À l'intérieur du musée, plusieurs très vastes et hautes galeries d'exposition sont équipées de plafonds en dalle de béton qui semblent flotter sous le toit. Ce procédé permet de moduler la lumière du jour, et de masquer au regard les conduits techniques et l'éclairage artificiel. Ce système, déjà utilisé par l'architecte pour le centre de Galice, assure un excellent éclairage naturel et artificiel, tout en présentant une simplicité apparente qui est la marque de l'ensemble de ce projet.

Siza donne une description «morphologique» de la Fondation Serralves: «Du corps principal partent vers le sud deux ailes asymétriques décrivant entre elles une cour, et un volume en forme de ‹L› orienté vers le nord, qui crée entre lui et le corps central une autre cour, dans les zones d'accès publics du bâtiment.»

Édifiée grâce à un budget à l'évidence confortable, la Fondation Serralves présente par ailleurs l'avantage d'être implantée dans un superbe parc, dont l'architecte a tenu compte en disposant stratégiquement un certain nombre de fenêtres qui délimitent avec art des vues soigneusement choisies.

< Galician Center for Contemporary Art,
Santiago de Compostela, Spain, 1988–93

Bauprogrammen umgeht, die notgedrungen vage formuliert sind, wie das der Fall war in Santiago und nun für die Serralves-Stiftung, antwortet Siza in typisch humorvoller Weise: »Was den Mangel an einem soliden Raumprogramm betrifft, so reagiere ich mit der japanischen Technik des Judo. Wenn man etwas nicht bekämpfen kann, akzeptiert man es. Fehlende Vorgaben erfordern einen flexiblen Entwurf. In modernen Kunstmuseen geht es heute zunehmend um die Organisation von Wechselausstellungen. Selbst in Museen mit sehr guten ständigen Sammlungen zeitgenössischer Kunst werden die Werke regelmäßig neu präsentiert. Sie nutzen sogar den Bestand, um daraus Sonderausstellungen zu machen. Die Aufgabe in derartigen Museen besteht also nicht in der Schaffung eines Szenarios mit besonderen Stücken, sondern in der Bereitstellung von Räumen, welche unterschiedliche Nutzungen erlauben, Flexibilität bieten und eine gewisse Neutralität. Damit ist nicht die Neutralität gemeint, die sich einige Kuratoren wünschen, nämlich Nicht-Architektur oder Leere. Ein Museumsbau sollte meiner Meinung nach einen eigenen Charakter haben und zu dem Milieu passen, in dem er steht. Er sollte aber auch in der Lage sein, fast alles in sich aufzunehmen.«[12]
In einiger Entfernung vom alten Stiftungsdomizil, einer in den 30er Jahren für den Grafen von Vizela erbauten Art-Déco-Villa, erhebt sich das neue Gebäude auf einem 3 Hektar großen Landschaftspark-Gelände. Der landschaftsarchitektonische Entwurf soll dazu beitragen, den Neubau in seine Umgebung einzubetten. In einigen der sehr weitläufigen, hohen Ausstellungshallen ist in die Decken eine Betonplatte integriert, welche knapp unter der Dachunterseite zu schweben scheinen. Diese Platten dienen dazu, moduliertes Tageslicht auf die Exponate zu werfen und bieten Sichtblenden für technische Leitungen und Beleuchtungskörper. Siza hatte das gleiche System schon im Galicischen Museum für Zeitgenössische Kunst eingesetzt. Es sorgt nicht nur für eine ausgezeichnete Tageslicht- und Kunstlichtbeleuchtung, sondern unterstützt auch die Schlichtheit des gesamten architektonischen Entwurfs.
Der Architekt gibt folgende »morphologische« Beschreibung des Neubaus der Serralves-Stiftung ab: »Vom Hauptbaukörper gehen in südlicher Richtung zwei asymmetrische, einen Hof umfassende Flügel aus sowie nach Norden ein L-förmiger Baukörper, der zusammen mit dem Hauptbau einen zweiten Hof bildet, und zwar im öffentlichen Eingangsbereich.« Für das Gebäude der Stiftung stand offensichtlich ein großzügiges Budget zur Verfügung. Der Bau genießt zudem den Vorzug, in einem wunderschön angelegten Park zu liegen. Der Architekt nutzte diese Situation, indem er mit einer Reihe strategisch plazierter Fenster sorgfältig ausgewählte »schöne Ausblicke« auf die Umgebung schuf.

EINE KIRCHE UND EIN HAUS

Zwei in jüngster Zeit fertiggestellte Bauten von Álvaro Siza verkörpern in besonderem Maße die Originalität und Kraft seiner Architektur. Der erste ist die Kirche Santa Maria in Marco de Canavezes

of the church in Marco, because it is in full use. It can be said that there were at least two individuals who brought this project to fruition. Siza is one, but the other is the young parish priest, Father Nuno Higino. An unassuming man with an engaging smile and brilliant eyes, Higino brings visitors to his church with an obvious, profound admiration for the building. It was his personal decision to call on Siza, and to invest himself fully in this very ambitious project. The austere, white form of the church stands out at a high point of this rather unattractive industrial town. A wide street, the Avenida Gago Coutinho, defines the lower boundary of the site, which rises over 2 meters near the entrance to the church. The dusty lot that was still in front of the doors of the church in 1998 is scheduled to be the site of the Parish Center. As Higino describes the future building, he gestures with palpable excitement to the still imaginary volumes, and as he turns again toward his church, an assistant has opened the temporary gray steel doors, offering a view straight toward the altar. Nothing prepares the visitor for the sight of the interior of this church. A 3 meter wide central aisle, with 400 wooden chairs designed by Siza on either side, leads to the altar, a solid block of marble also designed by the architect. Behind the altar, rising from the floor of the large white wall, are two "light chimneys," whose rectangular volume rises, until the impression of a "virtual" cross is created, "not drawn on the wall, but merely suggested by the light," as Father Higino says. The same light chimneys serve to light the mortuary chapel located one floor beneath the altar. To the left of the altar is a cross made, according to Siza's design, in gilt wood. But rather than the form of the Christian cross, the horizontal bar is here at the very top of the vertical one. In this work, the architect suggests not the cross but the body of Christ, suspended on an invisible cross.

At the entrance to the church, surprisingly, there are two large glass panels, an opening used in winter months on the right, and a window looking into the baptistery on the left. These openings

UNE ÉGLISE ET UNE MAISON

Deux bâtiments, récemment achevés, offrent une vision en concentré de l'originalité et de la puissance de l'œuvre de l'architecte. Le premier est l'église Santa Maria (Marco de Canavezes, 1990–96), à une demi-heure de voiture au nord de Porto. Le bâtiment lui-même n'a été achevé qu'en juin 1998, bien que manquent encore des équipements importants comme les portes de bronze de 10 mètres de haut, et surtout le centre paroissial prévu par l'architecte dans le cadre d'un complexe formant une petite place. Il est néanmoins possible de comprendre l'importance de cette réalisation, déjà ouverte au culte.

On peut dire que ce projet doit son existence à deux per-sonnalités. L'architecte bien sûr, mais aussi le jeune prêtre de la paroisse, le père Nuno Higino. Homme de grande modestie, au sourire engageant et au regard lumineux, il présente la nouvelle église à ses visiteurs avec une admiration profonde et authentique pour le bâtiment. C'est sur sa décision personnelle que l'on a fait appel à Siza, et il s'est totalement investi dans ce très ambitieux projet. La masse austère et blanche du lieu de culte se détache fortement sur l'un des points les plus élevés du panorama de cette ville industrielle sans grand intérêt. Une grande rue, l'Avenida Gago Coutinho, marque la limite inférieure du terrain, que l'entrée de l'église surplombe de plus de 2 mètres. C'est sur le terrain poussiéreux qui s'étend encore devant l'entrée que s'élèvera le centre paroissial.

En décrivant les futurs bâtiments, le prêtre parle avec une passion palpable des volumes encore imaginaires, et lorsqu'il se tourne vers l'église, un assistant ouvre les portes provisoires en acier pour offrir au visiteur une vue directe jusqu'à l'autel. Rien ne prépare à la vue de cet intérieur. Une allée centrale de 3 mètres de large, bordée de chaque côté de 400 sièges de bois dessinés par Siza, mène à l'autel, bloc de marbre massif également dû à l'architecte. Derrière l'autel, montant du sol devant le grand mur

(1990–96), eine halbe Autostunde nördlich von Porto. Im Juni 1998 war die Kirche noch immer nicht völlig fertiggestellt, da wichtige Elemente wie die 10 Meter hohen Bronzetüren noch fehlten; vor allem aber fehlte noch das Gemeindehaus, Teil eines Neubaukomplexes, der einen kleinen öffentlichen Platz bilden soll. Trotzdem läßt sich die Bedeutung der Kirche in Marco de Canavezes ermessen, da sie bereits genutzt wird.

Man kann sagen, daß in der Hauptsache zwei Personen dieses Projekt zustandegebracht haben: einerseits Siza und andererseits der junge Gemeindepfarrer, Pater Nuno Higino, ein bescheiden auftretender Mann mit gewinnendem Lächeln und wachen Augen. Higino führt Besucher mit offensichtlicher Bewunderung für Sizas Entwurf durch seine Kirche. Es war seine persönliche Entscheidung, Siza mit dem Neubau zu beauftragen und sich selbst mit diesem ehrgeizigen Vorhaben zu identifizieren. Der nüchterne weiße Baukörper der Kirche steht in auffälliger Position auf einer Anhöhe der ziemlich unattraktiven Industriestadt. Eine breite Straße, die Avenida Gago Coutinho, bildet die untere Begrenzung des Grundstücks, das über 2 Meter bis zum Vorplatz des Kirchenportals ansteigt. Auf dem staubigen Gelände, das sich im Juni 1998 noch vor dem Kirchentor erstreckte, soll das Gemeindehaus entstehen. Wenn Pater Higino das künftige Gebäude beschreibt, umreißt er mit spürbarer Begeisterung und weit ausholenden Gesten die noch imaginären Baukörper. Und als er sich wieder seiner Kirche zuwendet, hat ein Mitarbeiter inzwischen die provisorischen Stahltüren der Kirche geöffnet, so daß man geradewegs bis zum Altar blicken kann. Nichts bereitet den Besucher auf den Innenraum dieser Kirche vor. Ein 3 Meter breiter Mittelgang mit insgesamt 400 Holzstühlen zu beiden Seiten (von Siza entworfen) führt zum Altar, einem massiven Marmorblock, ebenfalls ein Entwurf von Siza. Hinter dem Altar erscheinen zwei schmale »Lichtkamine«, ausgehend vom Fußpunkt der großen weißen Wand, die den Eindruck eines »virtuellen« Kreuzes erwecken, das »nicht in die Wand eingezeichnet ist, sondern nur vom Lichteinfall hervorgerufen wird«, wie Pater Higino erklärt. Die Lichtkamine dienen auch der Belichtung der Grabkapelle unter dem Altar und dem Hauptschiff. Links vom Altar steht ein nach einem Entwurf von Siza gefertigtes vergoldetes Holzkreuz. Es hat hier nicht die Form des traditionellen Christuskreuzes, sondern der Querbalken befindet sich oben am Kreuzmast. Der Architekt suggeriert mit seinem Werk den Corpus Christi, der an einem unsichtbaren Kreuz aufgehängt wurde.

Am Eingang der Kirche befinden sich überraschenderweise zwei große verglaste Öffnungen. Die rechte wird in den Wintermonaten als Eingang genutzt, die linke bildet ein Fenster, durch das man in die Taufkapelle blickt. Diese Öffnungen symbolisieren die »Transparenz« der Kirche nach Meinung von Pater Higino. Der Pfarrer erklärt, daß viele Gestaltungsmerkmale des Gebäudes das Ergebnis eines fruchtbaren Dialogs mit dem Architekten seien. Es muß ein erstaunliches Zwiegespräch gewesen sein zwischen diesem modernen Kirchenmann und einem Architekten, der bekanntermaßen mit

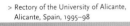
> Rectory of the University of Alicante, Alicante, Spain, 1995–98

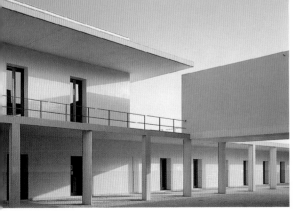

symbolize the "transparency" of the church for Father Higino, who explains that many of the features of the building are the result of a fruitful dialog with Siza. And what a surprising dialog it must have been, between this modern man of the church and the architect whose Communist sympathies are well known. Clad entirely in locally made tiles, the baptistery rises to the full height of one of the two entrance towers, flooded with light, the simple stone font precisely in its center.

Within, Father Higino motions to the visitor to sit in one very specific chair he has chosen, to the left of the nave. Here the long, low window that the visitor may have noticed without fully understanding suddenly takes on its meaning. When one is seated here, the crests of the neighboring mountains are framed like a long dialog between earth and sky. Finally, Father Higino guides the visitor to the small statue of the Virgin Mary, which stands to the right of the altar at ground level. He puts his hand around the shoulders of the polychrome wood sculpture and says, "This is Mary. She is not God. That is why she must be here, so that the parishioners may come and speak to her."

This great simplicity, which is that of both Higino and Siza, has resulted in a remarkable church, made with local traditional building techniques in order to keep expenses low. On the level below the nave, the still unfinished mortuary chapel completes the cycle of life begun at the entrance with the baptistery. Here, the visitor walks from dark spaces toward the light brought here by the light chimneys: from darkness into light.

Siza's Vieira de Castro House (1984–98), located in Famalicão, north of Porto, might not be considered one of his most important works, but as a recently completed project it does serve to underline the consistency of his creativity over time, his ability to adapt his work to particular sites, and his very personal approach to designing almost every detail of a structure. The fourteen year span from inception to completion in the case of the Vieira de Castro house is to some extent indicative of Siza's work

blanc, deux «cheminées de lumière» de forme rectangulaire s'élèvent jusqu'à créer une impression de croix «virtuelle», «non dessinée sur le mur, mais tout au plus suggérée par la lumière», précise le père Higino. La même cheminée de lumière sert à éclairer la chapelle mortuaire située un niveau plus bas que l'autel. À la gauche de celui-ci s'élève une croix en bois doré, également de Siza. Sa partie horizontale fixée au sommet de sa partie verticale suggère ainsi davantage le corps du Christ martyrisé que la croix chrétienne classique. À l'entrée de l'église, deux grands panneaux de verre surprennent: l'un est une porte utilisée en hiver et l'autre une baie qui donne sur les fonts baptismaux, installés à gauche. Pour le prêtre, ces ouvertures symbolisent la «transparence» de l'église, et il explique que beaucoup des caractéristiques du bâtiment sont nées d'un dialogue fructueux avec l'architecte. Les échanges entre l'homme d'église ouvert et l'architecte, dont les sympathies pro-communistes sont connues, ont dû réserver quelques surprises. Entièrement paré de carrelages de fabrication locale, le baptistère s'élève sur toute la hauteur de l'une des deux tours d'entrée, baigné de lumière, la très simple vasque de pierre disposée en son centre exact.

À l'intérieur, le père Higino convie le visiteur à s'asseoir dans un siège choisi par lui, à gauche de la nef. De là, la longue fenêtre basse que l'on a pu remarquer sans en comprendre véritablement le sens s'explique brusquement. Lorsque l'on s'assoit, les crêtes des montagnes voisines se retrouvent cadrées, comme pour illustrer un dialogue entre la terre et le ciel. Finalement, le prêtre guide le visiteur vers une petite statue de la Vierge Marie posée sur le sol, à droite de l'autel. Il place ses mains autour des épaules de la sculpture de bois polychrome et dit: «Voici Marie. Elle n'est pas Dieu. C'est pourquoi elle doit se trouver ici, afin que les paroissiens puissent venir et lui parler.»

La grande simplicité qui est celle de Siza et du père Higino a donné naissance à cette remarquable église, réalisée selon les techniques locales de construction pour en limiter le coût.

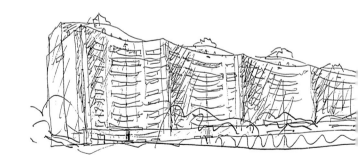

methods. Private houses are indeed not his priority, and a project such as this one, despite his very deep commitment to the design, had to wait on numerous occasions while his office worked on public buildings.

The industrial town of Famalicão appears only on detailed maps of Portugal, and it is certainly not remarkable, architecturally speaking. The Vieira de Castro house is clearly visible from the town, sitting on a hillside. The winding road that approaches it goes into the forest, and the visitor comes to an unusual, sculptural gate in Corten steel. Retaining walls in a roughly carved blond stone create the terrace where the house sits, looking to the south over the city. A rectangular swimming pool stretches forward from the house, prolonging the built form and articulating a pathway, to the right toward the main entrance to the house. Situated on the north side of the home, the entrance is reached by walking past a rough stone outcropping, which is allowed to disturb the linear path. Here, Siza's predilection for integrating his architecture into its setting, as he had already done in the Boa Nova Restaurant, again comes forward. Though this is quite a luxurious home, Álvaro Siza goes to some pains to make the entrance something other than grandiose.

Indeed, the Vieira de Castro house is a personal and private place, wanted by its owners, a couple with a young son, but outside and inside it is a pure expression of Álvaro Siza's talent. Almost every detail, including the built-in closets, was specifically designed for this home. White walls and a glorious bright light characterize the interior. An unusual downward curve in the wooden floor leads visitors from the entrance area toward the living room, where the stone fireplace, the furniture, and also the windows offering specifically framed views of the countryside, speak of the architect's presence. Although everything is designed for these clients in this place, the Vieira de Castro house is also a condensed resume of the wide-ranging talents of Álvaro Siza. Just as he has not signed the drawings on the walls of the restaurants

Sous la nef, la chapelle mortuaire, encore inachevée, représente l'achèvement du cycle de la vie, entamé dans le baptistère de l'entrée. Ici, le visiteur se déplace d'espaces sombres vers la lumière apportée par les cheminées. De l'obscurité vers la lumière.

La maison Vieira de Castro, située à Famalicão (1984–98) au nord de Porto, n'est sans doute pas l'une des plus importantes œuvres de Siza, mais, récemment achevée, elle illustre la constance de sa créativité au cours de sa carrière, sa capacité à s'adapter à des sites particuliers et son goût très personnel pour le soin porté aux moindres détails d'un projet. Dans le cas de cette maison, les quatorze années écoulées entre la conception et l'achèvement sont dans une certaine mesure révélatrices des méthodes de travail de Siza. Les résidences privées ne sont certes pas sa priorité, et un projet comme celui-ci, bien qu'il se soit profondément impliqué dans sa conception, a dû patienter à plusieurs reprises pendant que son agence travaillait sur des commandes publiques. La cité industrielle de Famalicão n'apparaît que sur les cartes détaillées du Portugal, et ne possède pas d'intérêt architectural particulier. La maison Vieira de Castro, à flanc de colline, s'aperçoit nettement de la ville. La route sinueuse qui la dessert traverse une forêt, et le visiteur tombe d'abord sur un étonnant portail sculptural en acier Corten. Des murs d'épaulement en pierre blonde grossièrement débitée délimitent la terrasse sur laquelle est implantée la maison, qui donne au sud et vers la ville. Une piscine rectangulaire se projette vers l'extérieur en prolongement du bâti et détermine à droite une allée qui mène vers l'entrée principale. Située sur la façade nord, celle-ci s'atteint en contournant un affleurement rocheux que l'on a laissé rompre la rectilinéarité du chemin. Ici, la prédilection de Siza pour l'intégration de l'architecture dans le site, comme pour le restaurant Boa Nova, s'affirme pleinement. Bien qu'il s'agisse d'une maison assez luxueuse, l'architecte explique qu'il a voulu une entrée qui ne soit pas grandiose.

den Kommunisten sympathisiert. Die Taufkapelle ist vollständig mit in der Region hergestellten Fliesen verkleidet und erhebt sich zur vollen Höhe des einen Eingangsturms. Sie ist lichtdurchflutet, und das schlichte Taufbecken steht exakt in ihrer Mitte.

Innen bedeutet Pater Higino dem Besucher, auf einem von ihm speziell ausgesuchten Stuhl links vom Mittelschiff Platz zu nehmen. Von hier aus erschließt sich dem Besucher die Bedeutung des langen niedrigen Fensters, das er vielleicht schon bemerkt hat, ohne seinen Sinn zu verstehen. Wenn man an dieser Stelle sitzt, werden die Silhouetten der nahen Berge vom Fenster eingerahmt wie ein »langer Dialog« zwischen Himmel und Erde. Schließlich führt Pater Higino den Besucher zu einer kleinen Statue der Jungfrau Maria, die rechts vom Altar auf dem Boden steht. Er legt seinen Arm um die Schultern der polychromen Holzfigur und sagt: »Das ist Maria. Sie ist nicht Gott, und deshalb muß sie hier stehen, damit die Gemeindemitglieder an sie herantreten und sie ansprechen können.«

Pater Higinos und Sizas gemeinsame Vorstellung von Klarheit und Schlichtheit hat einen bemerkenswerten Kirchenbau hervorgebracht, der mit traditionellen Bautechniken errichtet wurde, um die Kosten niedrig zu halten. Unter dem Hauptschiff befindet sich die Grabkapelle (1998 noch nicht fertiggestellt), die den mit dem Baptisterium am Kircheneingang begonnenen Lebenszyklus des Christen vollendet. Hier geht der Besucher von dunklen Raumbereichen zum Licht, das durch die Schächte hinter dem Altar einfällt: aus der Dunkelheit der Erde zum Licht des Himmels.

Das Einfamilienhaus Vieira de Castro (1984–98) in Famalicão nördlich von Porto ist vielleicht nicht Sizas wichtigstes Werk, dient aber, da es erst kürzlich fertiggestellt wurde, als Beleg für seine ausdauernde Schöpferkraft, für seine Fähigkeit, seine Bauten dem jeweiligen Standort anzupassen, und für seine ganz persönliche Auffassung, als Architekt fast jedes Detail selbst zu entwerfen. Die 14 Jahre zwischen der ersten Entwurfsskizze bis zum fertigen Haus Vieira de Castro sind bis zu einem gewissen Grade bezeichnend für Sizas Arbeitsweise. Einfamilienhäuser zählen in der Tat nicht zu seinen Prioritäten, und ein Projekt wie dieses mußte – obwohl Siza von keinerlei Zweifeln an seinem Entwurf geplagt wurde – mehrere Male ruhen, während er und seine Mitarbeiter mit dem Bau öffentlicher Gebäude beschäftigt waren.

Die mittelgroße Industriestadt Famalicão erscheint nur auf detaillierten Landkarten Portugals und ist in architektonischer Hinsicht ziemlich uninteressant. Das Haus Vieira de Castro ist von der Stadt aus gut sichtbar, da es an einem Hang steht. Die Zufahrtsstraße windet sich durch den Wald bis zu einem ungewöhnlichen, plastisch geformten Eingangstor aus Corten-Stahl. Stützmauern aus roh behauenem sandfarbenem Naturstein befestigen die Hangterrasse, auf der sich das Haus erhebt. Es ist nach Süden, zur Stadt hin, ausgerichtet. Ein rechteckiges Schwimmbecken bildet die Verlängerung des Baukörpers und begrenzt einen Fußweg, der zum an der Nordseite des Hauses befindlichen Haupteingang führt. Auf diesem Weg muß der Besucher eine schroffe Felsformation umgehen, wel-

of the Portuguese Pavilion, Álvaro Siza's interventions in the Vieira de Castro house are not the pretentious ramblings of an overbearing artist. They are subtle, both useful and aesthetic, blending into the whole to create what must indeed be considered a work of art.

Perhaps because it has been some time in design and construction, the Vieira de Castro house does not give one the feeling of a recently completed structure. Though it is decidedly modern, this house, blending into its rocky setting, has something personal yet timeless about it. It is a place where architecture, design, landscape architecture, and a sculptural sense of space and materials come together. These characteristics, coming together as they do in the Vieira de Castro house, as they do also in more important buildings such as the church in Marco or the Portuguese Pavilion, do much to define the complex creativity of one of the great architects of our time. Though it may not be fashionable to make such an affirmation, the Vieira de Castro house reminds the visitor of Álvaro Siza's own words, which might be his own provocative motto: "I would say that architecture is an art."

1 Interview with Álvaro Siza, Porto, May 24, 1998.
2 Ibid.
3 Ibid.
4 "Getting through turbulence," in: El Croquis, n° 68/69, El Croquis Editorial, Madrid, 1994.
5 Interview with Álvaro Siza, Porto, May 24, 1998.
6 Excerpt from Analysis of a Project – the Setúbal College of Education, in: Álvaro Siza, 1986–1995. Editorial Blau, Lisbon, 1995, p.9–10.
7 Interview with Álvaro Siza, Porto, May 24, 1998.
8 Ibid.
9 Ibid.
10 Ibid.
11 Interview with Álvaro Siza: "Centre galicien d'art contemporain," in: L'Architecture d'Aujourd'hui, 1994.
12 Interview with Álvaro Siza, Porto, May 24, 1998.

La maison Vieira de Castro est un lieu personnel et privé, voulu comme tel par ses propriétaires – un couple et son jeune fils. Mais à l'intérieur comme à l'extérieur, elle est l'expression pure du talent d'Álvaro Siza. Presque chaque détail, y compris les placards intégrés, a été spécialement pensé. L'intérieur se caractérise par des murs blancs et la richesse de l'éclatante lumière. Par une courbe dessinée dans le parquet de bois, on descend de l'entrée vers le séjour où la cheminée de pierre, le mobilier, mais également les fenêtres, qui offrent des vues très cadrées, parlent de la présence de l'architecte. Bien que tout ait été dessiné pour ces clients, cette maison est un résumé de ses multiples talents. De même qu'il n'a pas signé les dessins muraux du restaurant du Pavillon du Portugal, ses interventions ici n'ont rien à voir avec les prétentions envahissantes de certains artistes. Elles sont subtiles, à la fois esthétiques et utiles, et se fondent dans un tout pour créer ce qui pourrait à juste titre être qualifié d'œuvre d'art.

Peut-être parce qu'un certain temps s'est écoulé entre sa conception et sa construction, la maison Vieira de Castro ne donne pas le sentiment d'une réalisation qui vient juste d'être achevée. Bien qu'elle soit résolument moderne, cette maison, fondue dans son environnement rocheux, possède quelque chose de personnel et d'intemporel. C'est un lieu dans lequel l'architecture, le design, le paysage architecturé et un sens sculptural de l'espace et des matériaux se marient. Ces caractéristiques, réunies ici de la même manière que dans des réalisations plus importantes comme l'église de Marco ou le Pavillon du Portugal, éclairent grandement la créativité complexe de l'un des plus grands architectes de notre temps. Même si une telle affirmation n'est peut-être pas très à la mode, la maison Vieira de Castro rappelle les propres paroles d'Álvaro Siza, qui pourraient être sa provocante devise: «Je dirai que l'architecture est un art.»

1 Interview avec Álvaro Siza, Porto, le 24 mai 1998.
2 Ibid.
3 Ibid.
4 Getting through turbulence, in: El Croquis, n° 68/69, El Croquis Editorial, Madrid, 1994.
5 Interview avec Álvaro Siza, Porto, le 24 mai 1998.
6 Analysis of a Project. The Setúbal College of Education, in: Álvaro Siza, 1986–1995. Editorial Blau, Lisbonne, 1995, p. 9–10.
7 Interview avec Álvaro Siza, Porto, le 24 mai 1998.
8 Ibid.
9 Ibid.
10 Ibid.
11 Interview avec Álvaro Siza: Centre galicien d'art contemporain, in: L'Architecture d'Aujourd'hui, 1994.
12 Interview avec Álvaro Siza, Porto, le 24 mai 1998.

che die gerade Linie des Weges unterbricht. Hier wird erneut Sizas Vorliebe für die Einfügung seiner Bauten in die Topographie ihres Standortes ersichtlich, wie bereits beim Entwurf seines Restaurants Boa Nova. Obwohl dieses Einfamilienhaus ziemlich luxuriös ist, hat sich Álvaro Siza Mühe gegeben, den Eingangsbereich nicht allzu grandios erscheinen zu lassen.

Tatsächlich ist das Haus Vieira de Castro auf Wunsch seiner Besitzer – eines Ehepaars mit kleinem Sohn – ein sehr persönlicher, privater Ort, außen und innen aber ganz der Ausdruck von Álvaro Sizas Talent. Fast jedes Detail, einschließlich der Einbauschränke, wurde speziell für dieses Haus entworfen. Weiße Wände und eine herrliche Lichtfülle kennzeichnen die Innenräume. Ein leicht abfallender Holzkorridor führt den Ankommenden vom Eingangsbereich hinunter zum Wohnzimmer, wo der mit Natursteinen eingefaßte Kamin, die Möblierung und die spezielle Landschaftsausschnitte rahmenden Fenster die Handschrift des Architekten verraten. Obwohl, wie gesagt, alles für die Eigentümer entworfen und geschaffen wurde, gibt das Haus Vieira de Castro auch eine Zusammenfassung der breit gefächerten Begabung von Álvaro Siza. Wie im Restaurant des portugiesischen Expo-Pavillons, wo Siza seine an den Wänden reproduzierte Zeichnungen nicht signierte, stellt auch seine Innenausstattung des Hauses der Familie Vieira de Castro nicht die ausschweifenden Äußerungen eines großspurigen, von sich selbst allzu überzeugten Künstlers dar, sondern sie sind klug durchdacht, ebenso praktisch wie ästhetisch ansprechend und verschmelzen zu einem Ganzen, einem zu Recht so genannten Gesamtkunstwerk.

Das Haus Vieira de Castro vermittelt nicht den Eindruck, ein Neubau zu sein – vielleicht weil sich seine Fertigstellung über Jahre hinzog. Es ist zwar entschieden modern, schmiegt sich jedoch auf originelle und zugleich zeitlose Weise in seinen felsigen Grund. Es ist ein Ort, an dem sich Architektur, Design und Landschaftsarchitektur mit einem plastischen Raum- und Materialgefühl verbinden. Diese Merkmale, die Siza auch in seinen bedeutenderen, größeren Bauten wie der Kirche in Marco oder dem portugiesischen Expo-Pavillon verwirklicht hat, charakterisieren die Vielseitigkeit und Kreativität dieses großen Architekten unserer Zeit. Es mag nicht modern erscheinen, eine derartige Behauptung aufzustellen, aber das Haus Vieira de Castro erinnert den Besucher an Álvaro Sizas Worte, die sein eigenes provokantes Lebensmotto sein könnten: »Ich würde sagen, Architektur ist eine Kunst.«

1 Interview mit Álvaro Siza, Porto, 24. Mai 1998.
2 Ibid.
3 Ibid.
4 Getting through turbulence, in: El Croquis, Nr. 68/69, El Croquis Editorial, Madrid 1994.
5 Interview mit Álvaro Siza, Porto, 24. Mai 1998.
6 Analysis of a Project. The Setúbal College of Education, in: Álvaro Siza, 1986–1995. Editorial Blau, Lissabon 1995, S. 9–10.
7 Interview mit Álvaro Siza, Porto, 24. Mai 1998.
8 Ibid.
9 Ibid.
10 Ibid.
11 Interview mit Álvaro Siza: Centre galicien d'art contemporain, in: L'Architecture d'Aujourd'hui, 1994.
12 Interview mit Álvaro Siza, Porto, 24. Mai 1998.

Boa Nova Tea House and Restaurant, Leça da Palmeira, Portugal

Ocean Swimming Pool, Leça da Palmeira, Portugal

Alcino Cardoso House, Moledo do Minho, Portugal

Schlesisches Tor Urban Redevelopment, Kreuzberg, Berlin, Germany

Quinta da Malagueira Social Housing, Évora, Portugal

Borges & Irmão Bank, Vila do Conde, Portugal

Schilderswijk Social Housing Project, The Hague, The Netherlands

Faculty of Architecture of the University of Porto, Porto, Portugal

Superior School of Education, Setúbal, Portugal

Library of the University of Aveiro, Aveiro, Portugal

Galician Center for Contemporary Art, Santiago de Compostela, Spain

Reconstruction Plan for the Chiado Area, Lisbon, Portugal

Santa Maria Church and Parish Center, Marco de Canavezes, Portugal

Vitra International Office Furniture Factory, Weil am Rhein, Germany

Álvaro Siza Office, Porto, Portugal

Vieira de Castro House, Famalicão, Portugal

Portuguese Pavilion, Expo '98, Lisbon, Portugal

Rectory of the University of Alicante, Alicante, Spain

Boavista Building, Porto, Portugal

Serralves Foundation, Porto, Portugal

Santo Ovidio Estate, Douro Litoral, Portugal

Van Middelem-Dupont House, Oudenburg, Belgium

Boa Nova Tea House and Restaurant,
Leça da Palmeira, Portugal, 1958–1963

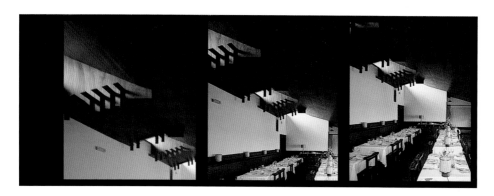

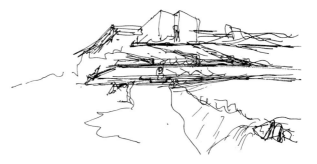

_A twenty minute drive in good traffic from the center of Porto, Leça da Palmeira is a largely industrial area on the Atlantic. Designed as part of a larger plan for the coastal area following a competition organized for this site by Fernando Távora, for whom Siza worked until 1958, the Boa Nova Tea House is integrated into the existing craggy rock formations. Walls extend from the actual built area in an irregular pattern, which at once acknowledges the natural setting and structures it, in harmony with the actual forms of the restaurant. Although the building is finished in stucco with a clay roof, giving it some connection to local traditions, it is not only resolutely modern, but also indicative of Álvaro Siza's future style. Siza leads the visitor up a stairway to a view of the open sea, before plunging into the darker interior spaces, where windows open onto the rock formations and the ocean. A craftsman-like attention to interior details, including the furniture and mahogany ceilings and floors, gives a warm atmosphere to the restaurant and tearoom, which brings to mind some of the work of Frank Lloyd Wright.

_À 20 minutes de voiture du centre de Porto, si la circulation est bonne, Leça de Palmeira est une zone d'urbanisation en grande partie industrielle en bordure de l'Atlantique. Conçu dans le cadre d'un plan plus vaste pour la zone côtière et à l'issue d'un concours organisé par Fernando Távora (pour lequel Siza a travaillé jusqu'en 1958), le Boa Nova s'intègre à des affleurements rocheux. Les murs se développent en harmonie avec les formes du restaurant à partir du bâti, selon un plan irrégulier qui tient compte du cadre naturel et de la structure. Le bâtiment, dont les murs sont enduits au plâtre et le toit recouvert de tuiles – traditions locales –, est à la fois résolument moderne, et annonce le style qui sera celui de Siza. L'architecte fait monter le visiteur par un escalier d'où l'on découvre le panorama infini de l'océan avant de le plonger dans des volumes intérieurs plus sombres, dont les fenêtres donnent sur les rochers et l'Atlantique. Une attention quasi artisanale aux détails de finition intérieure, dont le mobilier, les plafonds et les sols en acajou, confère une atmosphère chaleureuse à ce restaurant et salon de thé, qui rappelle certaines réalisations de Frank Lloyd Wright.

_20 Minuten Autofahrt vom Zentrum der Stadt Porto entfernt liegt Leça da Palmeira, ein großes Industriegebiet an der Atlantikküste. Das Teehaus und Restaurant Boa Nova gehört zu einem größeren Entwicklungsplan für diesen Küstenstreifen und ist Ergebnis eines Wettbewerbs, den Fernando Távora, für den Siza bis 1958 arbeitete, organisiert hatte. Sizas Bau fügt sich in die natürlichen Felsformationen des Geländes ein. Unregelmäßig sind Wände über den eigentlichen Baukörper hinaus errichtet, und zwar so, daß sie die natürliche Umgebung mit ihren Strukturen zugleich respektieren und gliedern, in Übereinstimmung mit den Formen des Restaurants. Obwohl es verputzt ist und ein Tonziegeldach hat, was die Verbindung zu traditionellen Bautechniken und -stilen der Gegend herstellt, ist es nicht nur entschieden modern, sondern auch richtungsweisend für Álvaro Sizas späteren Architekturstil. Siza führt den Besucher eine Treppe hinauf zu einem Aussichtspunkt mit Blick auf das offene Meer ehe er in die dunklen Innenräume vordringt, deren Fenster sich auf Felsformationen und das Meer hin öffnen. Handwerkliche Sorgfalt prägt die Details der Innenausstattung, einschließlich Möbeln, Mahagonidecken und -böden, die dem Restaurant und dem Teehaus eine warme Atmosphäre verleihen und an Interieurs von Frank Lloyd Wright denken lassen.

Ocean Swimming Pool,
Leça da Palmeira, Portugal, 1961–1966

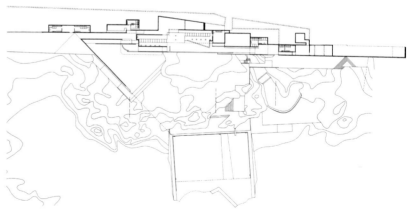

_Located within sight of the Boa Nova Restaurant, the swimming pool in Leça is one of Siza's more remarkable works. It takes into account not only the natural setting, with its rocky outcroppings, but also the man-made environment, represented here by a continuous cement wall that runs along the beach front. The visitor approaches the swimming pool by walking down a gently inclined ramp. A simple door leads to the dark wood changing rooms. A single band of bright exterior light enters this space at eye level, making a moment of adjustment to the lighting conditions inevitable. Plunged into an atmosphere that somehow evokes the intimacy of changing into a bathing suit, the visitor emerges into the full sun of the beach. Here, the walls built by Álvaro Siza define the swimming areas, as do the rock formations. In itself this combination of natural and modernist elements, this subtle presence that also affirms the identity of the architect is a real monument to the modern spirit. Whatever influences may have played on this project, it emerges as pure Siza.

_Visible du restaurant Boa Nova, la piscine de Leça est l'une des plus remarquables réalisations de Siza. Elle prend en compte non seulement le cadre naturel et ses excroissances rocheuses, mais également l'environnement tel qu'il a été modifié par l'homme, en l'occurrence un mur de ciment continu qui court le long de la plage. Le visiteur descend vers la piscine par une rampe en pente douce. Une simple porte ouvre sur les vestiaires plaqués de bois sombre. Une étroite baie horizontale aménagée au niveau des yeux éclaire l'intérieur d'une lumière éclatante qui force l'œil à s'accommoder. Plongé dans cette atmosphère qui évoque l'intimité du changement de vêtements, le visiteur émerge ensuite sur la plage, en plein soleil, où les murs édifiés par l'architecte et les rochers définissent les zones de natation. Cette combinaison d'éléments naturels et modernistes, cette présence subtile qui affirme l'identité de l'architecte font de cette piscine un authentique monument à l'esprit moderne. Quelles que soient les influences qui ont pu jouer sur ce projet, il relève du pur Siza.

_Das in Sichtweite des Restaurants Boa Nova gelegene Meeresschwimmbad in Leça da Palmeira ist eines von Sizas bemerkenswertesten Werken. Der Entwurf berücksichtigt nicht nur die natürliche Topographie mit zahlreichen Felsformationen, sondern auch die von Menschenhand geschaffenen Elemente, hier eine am Strand entlang verlaufende durchgehende Zementmauer. Die Badegäste gelangen über eine Rampe in die Badeanlage und durch eine einfache Tür in die holzverkleideten Umkleideräume. Ein einziges in Augenhöhe angebrachtes Fensterband läßt Tageslicht in diese Räume einfallen, und das Auge benötigt eine Zeitlang um sich auf die Lichtverhältnisse einzustellen. Aus den Umkleideräumen tritt der Besucher hinaus auf den sonnendurchglühten Strand. Hier umfassen die von Siza entworfenen Mauern im Verbund mit den natürlichen Felsen die Schwimmbecken. Diese Kombination natürlicher und moderner Elemente, diese behutsamen Eingriffe in das Vorgefundene sind charakteristisch für Sizas Architektur und ein Denkmal für den Geist der Moderne.

Alcino Cardoso House,
Moledo do Minho, Portugal, 1971–1973

Alcino Cardoso House (rural complex),
Moledo do Minho, Portugal, 1988

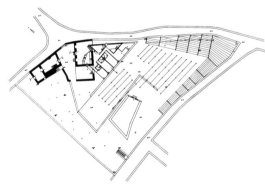

_In a sense, the intervention of Álvaro Siza in the case of this holiday residence prefigures what he did more recently in the Chiado district of Lisbon. By adding a modern house to existing farm structures in such a way as to retain the rural atmosphere of the whole, the architect affirms his presence while accepting the reality of the existing architecture. Although his metal and glass addition to the original house, apparently designed with the idea of a hinge in mind, is discernible from the exterior, his use of a local, rough stone for a supporting wall makes the whole blend into its environment. The same can be said of the swimming pool, situated below the added section of the house on this hillside property.

_En un sens, l'intervention d'Álvaro Siza sur cette résidence de vacances préfigure ce qu'il a réalisé plus récemment dans le quartier du Chiado, à Lisbonne. En ajoutant une maison moderne à des bâtiments agricoles préexistants sans porter atteinte à l'atmosphère rurale de l'ensemble, l'architecte affirme sa présence tout en acceptant la réalité du bâti antérieur. Si l'extension en verre et métal de la maison d'origine, apparemment dessinée selon un principe de charnière, est bien visible de l'extérieur, l'utilisation de la pierre locale brute pour un mur de soutènement permet à l'ensemble de se fondre dans son environnement. Il en est de même de la piscine, située sous l'extension, à flanc de colline.

_In gewissem Sinne nimmt Álvaro Sizas Umbau und Erweiterung dieses Ferienhaus-Ensembles vorweg, was er in jüngerer Zeit im Chiado-Bezirk von Lissabon geschaffen hat. Indem er ein modernes Haus an ein altes Bauernhaus anbaute und dabei doch den ländlichen Charakter des Anwesens wahrte, bekräftigte der Architekt seine eigene Präsenz und respektierte die bestehende Architektur. Seine Erweiterung des Altbaus aus Glas und Stahl – offenbar mit dem Gedanken an ein Scharniergelenk entworfen – ist zwar von außen augenfällig, die Stützmauer aus roh behauenem Stein aus einem lokalen Steinbruch läßt das Ensemble allerdings wieder mit seiner Umgebung verschmelzen, wie das Schwimmbecken am Hang unterhalb des Anbaus.

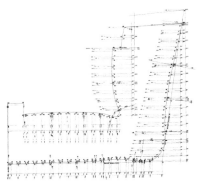

_Apparently influenced to some extent by the work of Hans Scharoun, **Bonjour Tristesse**, an unexpected low-cost housing complex, was designed by Álvaro Siza in the context of the International Building Exhibition (IBA, 1987) in Berlin, and occupies a large corner site. The design was modified to take into account economic considerations imposed by the developer, and the gray building seems to carry its name rather well. Álvaro Siza also built two smaller buildings – a kindergarten and an old age home – in the Kreuzberg district of Berlin in the 1980s. On a much smaller scale than Bonjour Tristesse, these buildings, both of which are located on the same piece of land, despite being distinct in their function and design, are more reminiscent of Siza's work in Portugal than the IBA block, with their white stucco facades and asymmetrical window patterns.

_Apparemment influencé dans une certaine mesure par l'œuvre de Hans Scharoun, **Bonjour Tristesse** est un curieux ensemble de logements économiques conçu par Álvaro Siza dans le cadre de l'Exposition internationale de la Construction (IBA, 1987) à Berlin. Implanté sur un vaste terrain d'angle, le projet a été modifié pour prendre en compte certaines contraintes économiques imposées par le promoteur, et cet immeuble gris semble porter assez bien son nom. Siza a également construit sur un même terrain du quartier berlinois de Kreuzberg, au cours des années 80, deux immeubles de fonction et de plans distincts: un jardin d'enfants et une maison pour personnes âgées. À une échelle beaucoup plus réduite que Bonjour Tristesse, ces deux réalisations aux façades enduites en blanc et aux fenêtres asymétriques rappellent davantage les réalisations portugaises de Siza que l'immeuble de l'IBA.

_Álvaro Siza ließ sich beim Entwurf des Sozialwohnungsblocks **Bonjour Tristesse** offenbar bis zu einem gewissen Grad von der Architektur Hans Scharouns leiten. Diese Eckbebauung entstand im Rahmen der Internationalen Bauausstellung in Berlin (IBA, 1987). Siza mußte den Entwurf überarbeiten, um den vom Bauträger vorgegebenen engen finanziellen Rahmen nicht zu sprengen, und das graue Gebäude macht seinem Namen alle Ehre. Siza baute in den 80er Jahren zwei weitere Gebäude, einen Kindergarten und ein Seniorenheim im gleichen Block in Kreuzberg. Diese beiden Bauten sind viel kleiner als Bonjour Tristesse und entsprechend ihrer jeweiligen Funktion ganz unterschiedlich gestaltet: sie erinnern mit ihren weißen Putzfassaden und der asymmetrischen Fenstergliederung eher an Sizas Bauten in Portugal als an das IBA-Haus.

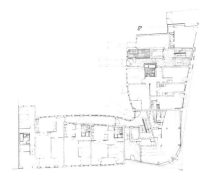

Schlesisches Tor Urban Redevelopment,
Kreuzberg, Berlin, Germany
Bonjour Tristesse Apartment Building, Schlesisches Tor, 1980–1984
Kindergarten, Schlesische Strasse, 1986–1988
Old Age Home, Falckensteinstrasse, 1987–1988

_Two interior views and an image of the facade of the **Old Age Home**, together with a floor plan and an elevation, show how the apparent simplicity of Siza's architecture in fact involves a subtle interplay of complex spaces.

_Deux vues intérieures, un plan d'étage et une élévation de la façade de la **maison de retraite** montrent que la simplicité apparente de l'architecture de Siza implique en fait l'interrelation subtile d'espaces complexes.

_Zwei Innenansichten und ein Bild der Fassade des **Seniorenheims** zeigen, zusammen mit einem Grundriß und einem Aufriß, daß die scheinbare Schlichtheit von Sizas Architektur in Wirklichkeit ein subtiles Wechselspiel komplexer Räumlichkeiten darstellt.

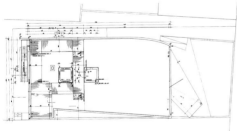

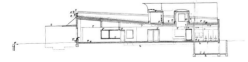

_Located on the same lot as the Old Age Home, the **Kindergarten** finds a certain resonance with neighboring buildings despite obvious stylistic differences. The architecture here makes no specific exterior reference to its function.

_Situé sur la même parcelle de terrain que la maison de retraite, le **jardin d'enfants** entretient certains rapports avec les constructions voisines, malgré des différences stylistiques évidentes. L'architecture ne fait ici aucune référence extérieure explicite à sa fonction.

_Der auf dem gleichen Grundstück wie das Seniorenheim errichtete **Kindergarten** weist trotz offensichtlicher stilistischer Unterschiede Anklänge an die umgebenden Bauten auf. Die äußere architektonische Gestaltung nimmt allerdings keinen besonderen Bezug auf die Funktion des Gebäudes.

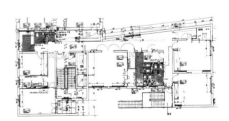

Quinta da Malagueira Social Housing,
Évora, Portugal, 1977–1995

Quinta da Malagueira Social Housing, Évora, Portugal

_Long an important Roman military center, Évora, located in fertile low hills 130 kilometers south east of Lisbon, is a well-preserved walled city of about 40,000 inhabitants. Designed and built in phases since 1977, Siza's Quinta da Malagueira is a significant effort to bring decent modern housing to a relatively poor population. With a total of 1,200 units built, and the hope that, one day, planned municipal infrastructure can also be completed, the Quinta da Malagueira offers pleasant individual homes with small courtyards. Although aligned in rows, the houses have a certain individuality, because of the various configurations envisaged by the architect, but also because residents have taken it on themselves to work on the courtyards in various ways. Surrounded by lush green space and divided into several areas, the Évora housing project can be judged as a significant success, countering the preconceived modernist image of faceless, prefabricated mass housing.

_Jadis important centre militaire romain, Évora, située dans une fertile région vallonnée à 130 km au sud-est de Lisbonne, est une cité de 40 000 habitants environ, entourée de murailles assez bien préservées. Projetée et construite en plusieurs phases à partir de 1977, la Quinta da Malagueira manifeste la volonté concrète d'offrir des logements modernes décents à une population relativement défavorisée. Avec ses 1 200 unités d'habitation construites, et l'espoir qu'un jour les infrastructures urbaines seront achevées, la Quinta offre d'agréables maisons individuelles à petites cours privées. Bien qu'alignées en rangées, elles ne possèdent pas moins une certaine individualité du fait des diverses configurations prévues par l'architecte, mais également parce que chaque habitant a aménagé sa cour à sa manière. Entouré d'abondants espaces verts et divisé en plusieurs quartiers, cet important projet social peut être considéré comme une réussite significative, loin de l'image moderniste préconçue de logements préfabriqués sans visage et construits en série.

_Die Kleinstadt Évora mit knapp 40 000 Einwohnern liegt in einer fruchtbaren, hügeligen Landschaft ca. 130 km südöstlich von Lissabon. Die gut erhaltene, befestigte Stadt war über lange Zeit ein Militärstützpunkt der Römer. Sizas Sozialbausiedlung Quinta da Malagueira, die seit 1977 entworfen und gebaut wird, stellt einen bedeutenden Beitrag zur Versorgung einer relativ armen Bevölkerung mit bescheidenen, modernen Wohnungen dar. 1 200 Wohneinheiten sind fertiggestellt, und es besteht die Hoffnung, daß der neue Stadtteil mit der Fertigstellung der geplanten städtischen Einrichtungen und Infrastruktur eines Tages rundherum angenehme Eigenheime mit kleinen Höfen bieten wird. Obwohl es sich um Zeilenbauten handelt, wirken sie dennoch individuell, weil der Architekt sie unterschiedlich entworfen hat, und die Bewohner die Innenhöfe nach eigenem Geschmack gestaltet haben. Umgeben von üppigem Grün und in verschiedene Bereiche aufgeteilt, kann die Siedlung als sehr gelungen bewertet werden, da sie das Vorurteil widerlegt, eine moderne Sozialbausiedlung zu errichten bedeute eine gesichtslose vorgefertigte Massenproduktion von Wohnblöcken.

Borges & Irmão Bank,
Vila do Conde, Portugal, 1978 (phase 1),
1982–1986 (phase 2)

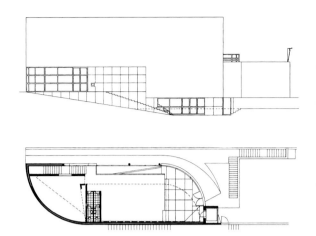

_Álvaro Siza was awarded the 1988 Mies van der Rohe Prize by the European Community for his work on this bank, which is located in an historic city center near the Matriz Church and the Santa Clara Convent. Mixing rounded and rectilinear elements, blank and glazed surfaces, the architect succeeds in inserting a visibly modern building that is in harmony with its surroundings. Interior detailing, including numerous surfaces clad in white marble, displays a variety of the articulations of form and materials that Siza enjoys. The alternation of windows, artificial light sources, and solid volumes is almost symphonic in its complexity, for example in the stairway leading up from the banking hall. The Borges & Irmão Bank would appear to be a project ideally suited to the subtlety and intricacy of which Siza's architecture is capable, while remaining respectful of an urban environment and of the client's needs.

_En 1988, Álvaro Siza a reçu le Prix Mies van der Rohe de la Communauté Européenne pour cette banque, située dans un centre historique non loin de l'église de la Matriz et du couvent de Santa Clara. Associant des éléments rectilignes ou arrondis à des surfaces neutres et vitrées, l'architecte a réussi à insérer harmonieusement cet immeuble visiblement moderne dans son environnement. L'exécution des espaces intérieurs, aux nombreuses surfaces recouvertes de marbre blanc, témoigne de la variété d'articulation de formes et de matériaux qu'apprécie l'architecte. L'alternance de fenêtres, de sources d'éclairage artificiel et de volumes pleins est d'une complexité quasi symphonique, par exemple dans l'escalier qui part du grand hall de la banque. Cette réalisation est l'image idéale de la subtilité et de la complexité dont l'architecture de Siza est capable, tout en restant respectueuse de son environnement urbain et des besoins du client.

_Für seinen Entwurf zu diesem Bankgebäude erhielt Álvaro Siza 1988 den Mies-van-der-Rohe-Preis der Europäischen Gemeinschaft. Das Bankhaus befindet sich in der Altstadt unweit der Matriz-Kirche und des Santa Clara-Klosters. Mit runden und eckigen Formen, verputzten und gläsernen Fassadenteilen gelang es dem Architekten, ein sichtlich modernes Gebäude zu schaffen, das im Einklang mit seiner Umgebung steht. Die Innenausstattung mit zahlreichen weißen Marmorflächen zeigt eine Auswahl des Formenrepertoires und der Materialien, die Siza bevorzugt. Der Wechsel von Fenstern mit Kunstlichtquellen und massiven Volumen erscheint wie eine komplexe architektonische Symphonie, beispielsweise bei der Treppenkonstruktion in der Schalterhalle. Die Borges & Irmão Bank zeigt die Subtilität und minutiös ausgearbeitete Komplexität von Sizas Architektur sowie seine Fähigkeit, die städtische Umgebung und die Bedürfnisse des Auftraggebers zu berücksichtigen.

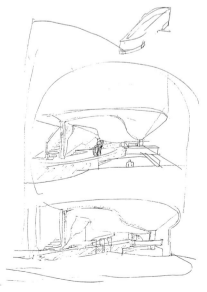

Schilderswijk Social Housing Project,
The Hague, The Netherlands,
1983–1988; 1989–1993

_The Schilderswijk social housing project was developed in two phases in a rundown area of The Hague. Although these brick-clad structures (red and pale bricks are employed) appear to be extremely rigorous and rectilinear in their design, they call not only on local tradition but also on the results of discussions with the residents. Brick is indeed a material that is very frequently used in The Netherlands. By combining it with a familiar scale, often seen in Dutch cities, and which in some elevations recalls individual row houses, Siza succeeded in giving an essentially repetitive design a connection to its specific location. The perceived rectilinearity is indeed broken to some extent in the corners of the units, providing spaces for shops. As was the case in Berlin, where he built several structures, Siza has also completed other work in The Hague, including two houses in the Van der Venne Park (with Mecanoo).

_Le projet de logements sociaux de Schilderswijk – une zone délabrée de La Haye – s'est déroulé en deux phases. Si ces constructions parées de brique (rouge sombre et pâle) paraissent de dessin extrêmement raide et rigoureux, elles ne s'en appuient pas moins sur les traditions locales et sur de nombreux échanges avec leurs futurs résidents. La brique est un matériau très courant aux Pays-Bas. En l'associant à une échelle familière, fréquente dans les villes néerlandaises, et qui dans certaines élévations rappelle des alignements de maisons individuelles, Siza a réussi à créer un motif essentiellement répétitif en rapport avec la spécificité du lieu. La rectilinéarité est en fait rompue dans une certaine mesure à l'angle des bâtiments pour laisser place à des commerces. Comme à Berlin, où il a construit plusieurs immeubles, Siza a également signé d'autres réalisations à La Haye, dont deux maisons dans le Van der Venne Park (avec Mecanoo).

_Das Schilderswijk-Wohnsiedlungsprojekt wurde in zwei Bauphasen in einem heruntergekommenen Stadtgebiet von Den Haag realisiert. Die Gestaltung und Gliederung dieser Häuser mit roten und blaßgelben Klinkerfassaden erscheinen streng und linear, sie folgen jedoch den ortsüblichen Bautraditionen und sind auch das Ergebnis von Gesprächen mit den Bewohnern. Backsteinklinker werden in den Niederlanden häufig beim Bau von Häusern eingesetzt. Mit einer aus anderen Orten des Landes vertrauten Maßstäblichkeit, die an einigen Fassaden den Eindruck von individuellen Reihenhäusern erweckt, stellt diese Siedlung mit ihrem sich wiederholenden Formenkanon eine gelungene Verbindung zu ihrem Standort her. Die weitgehend durchgängige Linearität des Komplexes wird an einigen Ecken aufgebrochen, so daß sich Platz für Geschäfte bietet. Wie schon in Berlin hat Siza auch in Den Haag eine Reihe von Wohnhäusern realisiert, unter anderen zwei Häuser im Van der Venne Park (in Zusammenarbeit mit Mecanoo).

Faculty of Architecture of the University of Porto,
Porto, Portugal, 1987–1993

_Based on a preliminary program established by the Rectory of the University of Porto, the faculty is set on a terraced site quite high above the estuary of the Douro River, which runs through Porto. This facility covers a total area of 87,000 square meters. Although there are apparently four free-standing pavilions at the southern end of the site, these classroom buildings are in fact connected 3 meters below grade by a long, narrow corridor. The largest building, located to the north, contains offices, auditoriums, an exhibition space that has yet to be used, and a library. As Siza says, "The structure converges westward, clearly marking the main entryway to the triangular enclosure at the heart of the installations." Articulated by a series of rusticated stone walls, the complex is intricately related to two other structures, the renovated Quinta da Póvoa House and the Carlos Ramos Pavilion, a Siza classroom building, erected prior to the construction of the main group. Although Siza would have preferred to have more circulation areas in the Faculty, outdoor areas such as the central, triangular courtyard, and the connecting paths give an impression of a generous space.

_Dans le cadre d'un programme préliminaire établi par le rectorat de l'Université de Porto, la faculté a été implantée sur un site en terrasse qui domine d'assez haut l'estuaire du Douro, le fleuve qui traverse Porto. Elle couvre une surface totale de 87 000 m². Au sud du terrain, les quatre pavillons de salles de cours apparemment indépendants sont en fait reliés par un long corridor étroit, à 3 mètres sous le niveau de la cour centrale. Au nord, le bâtiment le plus vaste contient des bureaux, un auditorium, un espace d'exposition non encore utilisé et une bibliothèque. Comme le commente Siza: «La structure est orientée vers l'ouest pour clairement marquer l'entrée principale de l'enclos triangulaire en plein cœur de ces installations.» Articulé sur une série de murs en pierre rustiquée, le complexe est étroitement relié à deux autres constructions, la maison Quinta da Póvoa rénovée et le Pavillon Carlos Ramos, un bâtiment de salles de cours dessiné par Siza et implanté en avant du groupe des bâtiments principaux. Bien que l'architecte eût préféré pouvoir créer davantage d'espaces de circulation dans la faculté, les zones extérieures, comme la cour triangulaire centrale, et les chemins qui y conduisent donnent une impression de générosité d'espace.

_Entsprechend einem ausgearbeitetem Programm, das vom Dekanat der Universität Porto aufgestellt wurde, steht der Fakultätskomplex auf einem terrassierten Hanggrundstück in einiger Höhe über der Mündung des Douro, der durch die Stadt Porto fließt. Überbaut wurde eine Fläche von insgesamt 87 000 m². Obwohl die vier Pavillons am südlichen Ende des Geländes als separate, freistehende Konstruktionen erscheinen, sind sie durch einen langen, schmalen Korridor miteinander verbunden, der 3 Meter unter Niveau des zentralen Campus liegt. Der größte, nördlichste Pavillon enthält Büros, Hörsäle, einen bislang noch ungenutzten Ausstellungsraum und eine Bibliothek. Siza erläutert: »Der Bau verjüngt sich in westlicher Richtung und markiert so deutlich den Hauptzugang zum dreieckigen Hof im Zentrum des Komplexes.« Die Gesamtanlage wird durch eine Reihe von rohen Natursteinmauern gegliedert und steht in engem Zusammenhang mit zwei weiteren Bauten, dem restaurierten Landsitz Quinta da Póvoa und dem Carlos Ramos Pavillon, einem von Siza erbauten Gebäude mit Seminar- und Unterrichtsräumen, das zeitlich vor dem Hauptkomplex realisiert wurde. Siza hätte es vorgezogen, mehr Begegnungsflächen im Innern des Fakultätsgebäudes unterzubringen, Außenbereiche wie der zentrale dreieckige Hof und Verbindungspfade sorgen allerdings dafür, daß das Ensemble aufgelockert und großzügig wirkt.

_Built very close to the site of the School of Architecture to be used during the period of construction, the small **Carlos Ramos Pavilion** presents some anthropomorphic features, and features a staircase in the entrance that brings to mind Michelangelo's stairway for the Laurentian Library in Florence. To the right, a site plan for the entire school.

_Édifié très près du site de l'École d'architecture, pour servir pendant la période de chantier, le petit **Pavillon Carlos Ramos** présente certains traits anthropomorphiques. Dans l'entrée, son escalier fait penser à celui de Michel-Ange pour la bibliothèque Laurentienne à Florence. À droite, plan complet de l'École d'architecture.

_Direkt neben dem Standort des Neubaus der Architekturfakultät und zur Nutzung während dessen Bauzeit bestimmt, steht der kleine **Carlos Ramos Pavillon**, der einige anthropomorphe Züge aufweist und dessen Eingangstreppe an Michelangelos Treppe in der Biblioteca Laurenziana in Florenz erinnert. Rechts ein Lageplan der gesamten Fakultät.

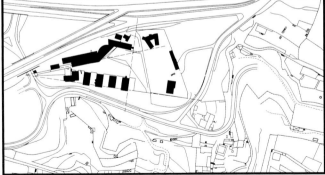

Superior School of Education,
Setúbal, Portugal, 1986–1994

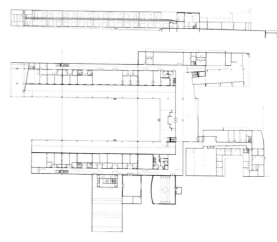

_Located on the northern shore of a deep estuary formed by the Sado, Marateca, and São Martinho rivers, Setúbal served as a royal residence during the reign of King John II (1481–95). Today Portugal's third most important port, Setúbal has a population of about 80,000. Located on the hill that dominates the downtown area, the Superior School of Education has an almost park-like setting, surrounded by trees and grass. An approach path is today painted in a warm red that recalls the architecture of Luis Barragán, whom Siza admires. The school is laid out in a basic U-plan, with a central grass courtyard and a single large tree almost directly located in the central axis of the project. Within, the pleasant, open classrooms open out onto the courtyard, while other less expected features, such as an anthropomorphic volume near the main entrance, and an often photographed stairway leading to the second floor, proclaim that this is indeed a work of Álvaro Siza.

_Située sur la rive nord d'un profond estuaire formé par le Sado, la Marateca et le São Martinho, Setúbal a servi de résidence royale sous le règne de Jean II (1481–95). Aujourd'hui troisième port du Portugal, la ville compte 80 000 habitants environ. Sur une colline qui domine les quartiers du centre, l'École normale supérieure entourée d'arbres et de pelouses semble implantée dans un parc. Accessible par une voie peinte d'un rouge chaleureux rappelant l'architecture de Luis Barragán que Siza admire, l'École se déploie selon un plan en «U», avec une cour centrale gazonnée, ornée d'un seul et unique grand arbre qui pousse pratiquement dans l'axe central du projet. À l'intérieur, d'agréables salles d'enseignement donnent sur la cour, tandis que d'autres éléments plus inattendus, comme le volume anthropomorphique à l'entrée principale et l'escalier souvent photographié qui mène à l'étage, confirment qu'il s'agit bien d'une œuvre d'Álvaro Siza.

_Die Stadt Setúbal, gelegen an der breiten Mündungsbucht des Rio Sado, war während der Regierungszeit König Johanns II. (1481–95) königliche Residenzstadt. Setúbal ist heute Portugals drittgrößter Hafen und hat etwa 80 000 Einwohner. Auf der Anhöhe über der Altstadt befindet sich das Ausbildungsinstitut für Lehrer in einem parkähnlichen Gelände, umgeben von Bäumen und Rasenflächen. Ein Zugangsweg in warmem Rot erinnert an die Architektur von Luis Barragán, den Siza sehr verehrt. Das Gebäude ist auf U-förmigem Grundriß errichtet und umschließt einen zentralen, grasbewachsenen Hof mit einem großen alten Baum, der fast genau auf der Mittelachse des Gebäudes steht. Die freundlichen, hellen Unterrichtsräume öffnen sich zum Hof hin, während andere, überraschendere Elemente das Gebäude als Werk Álvaro Sizas ausweisen, zum Beispiel ein anthropomorpher Baukörper am Haupteingang und eine vielfach fotografierte Treppe, die ins Obergeschoß führt.

Library of the University of Aveiro,
Aveiro, Portugal, 1988–1995

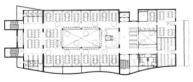

_Located at the mouth of the Rio Vouga south of Porto along the A1 highway, which leads to Lisbon, Aveiro has a population of about 35,000. A plan for the city center was carried out in 1962–65 by Fernando Távora, and the University of Aveiro was founded in 1973. Located not far from the city, looking out on nearby salt marshes, the University has a relatively strict building code, which calls for brick cladding and limestone trim, a code that Álvaro Siza respected with brio. Aside from these materials, which are unexpected in the case of Siza, the undulating facade facing the marshes and the elevated portico are the most outstanding features of the building. Within, a clear layout, good lighting, and a wealth of carefully crafted details, from handrails to library furniture, make this an exceptionally pleasant place in which to work. In a typical gesture the architect frames views out onto the marshes, offering some alternative to the sight of open books. Just down the road from this library, Siza has also designed a tall thin water tower, which almost resembles a Minimalist sculpture in concrete.

_Situé à l'embouchure du Rio Vouga, au sud de Porto, le long de l'autoroute A1 qui mène à Lisbonne, Aveiro compte environ 35 000 habitants. Le plan de restructuration du centre ville a été mis au point en 1962–65 par Fernando Távora, et l'Université de Aveiro a été fondée en 1973. Non loin de la ville, donnant sur des marais salants avoisinants, l'Université est soumise à un règlement de construction relativement strict qui exige des parements de brique et de pierre, contrainte que Siza a respectée avec brio. En dehors de ces matériaux, inattendus chez l'architecte, la façade ondulée face aux marais et le haut portique en sont les éléments les plus remarquables. À l'intérieur, un plan lisible, un éclairage étudié et une multiplicité de détails soigneusement mis en œuvre – des rampes au mobilier de la bibliothèque – font que ce bâtiment offre un cadre de travail extrêmement agréable. À sa manière typique, Siza a cadré des vues vers les marais, qui changent de celle des livres ouverts. En bas de la route qui mène à la bibliothèque, il a également dessiné un château d'eau élancé qui ressemble presque à une sculpture minimaliste en béton.

_Die Stadt Aveiro mit etwa 35 000 Einwohnern liegt an der Mündung des Rio Vouga südlich von Porto an der Autobahn A1 nach Lissabon. Ein Stadtentwicklungsplan für die Innenstadt wurde in den Jahren 1962–65 von Fernando Távora aufgestellt, die Universität von Aveiro 1973 gegründet. Die Universität entstand nicht weit von der Stadt mit Blick über die nahegelegenen Salzsümpfe. Álvaro Siza mußte bei der architektonischen Gestaltung strengen Bauauflagen folgen, die zum Beispiel Klinkerverblendungen mit Kalksteineinfassungen verlangten, was er »mit Bravour« erfüllte. Außer diesen Materialien, die in Sizas Architektur unerwartet erscheinen, sind die geschwungene Westfassade zu den Salzsümpfen hin und der erhöhte Portikus die markanten Merkmale des Bibliotheksgebäudes. Innen machen eine klare Raumaufteilung, gute Beleuchtung und eine Fülle handwerklich hochwertiger Details (von Handläufen bis zur Bibliothekseinrichtung) den Bau zu einem angenehmen Arbeitsplatz. Auf eine für ihn typische Weise rahmt der Architekt Ausblicke auf das Marschland mit Fenstern ein und bietet damit eine Abwechslung zu aufgeschlagenen Büchern. Nicht weit von der Universitätsbibliothek hat Siza an der gleichen Straße einen hohen, schlanken Wasserturm entworfen, der wie eine minimalistische Betonplastik anmutet.

Galician Center for Contemporary Art,
Santiago de Compostela, Spain, 1988–1993

_This 7,000 square meter museum building is set on a triangular lot in the midst of the 17th century Santo Domingo de Bonaval convent. Clad in granite, like many local buildings, it seeks to respond in a modern yet appropriate way to its surroundings, in harmony with the neighboring historic structures. Siza says, "I can't say exactly why, but I am convinced, because I have visited Santiago intensively, that the building seems very natural in this urban landscape." Its long, often blank facades respond to the nearby rough stone walls. As the architect points out, there were neither collections nor a curator when he received this commission, requiring him to devise a flexible solution which he found in the shape of a plan made up of two overlapping L-shaped volumes. Both outside and in, an emphasis has been placed on a purity of line. The white interiors, with Greek marble flooring in the public areas, are rendered all the more pure by the use of suspended ceilings, which conceal security systems and lighting sources, both natural and artificial.

_Ce musée de 7 000 m² s'élève sur un terrain triangulaire au centre de l'enclos du couvent Santo Domingo de Bonaval (XVIIe siècle). Recouvert de granit, comme beaucoup de bâtiments locaux, il semble répondre d'une manière moderne, mais appropriée néanmoins, à son environnement, en harmonie avec les bâtiments qui l'entourent. Siza déclare: «Je ne peux dire exactement pourquoi, mais parce que j'ai visité Saint-Jacques en détail, je suis convaincu que le bâtiment trouve très naturellement sa place dans ce paysage urbain.» Ses longues façades, souvent aveugles, répondent aux murs de pierre brute avoisinants. L'architecte fait remarquer qu'il n'y avait ni collections ni musée lorsqu'il a été chargé de ces travaux, et qu'il a donc dû trouver une solution souple, en l'espèce deux volumes en «L» se chevauchant. À l'extérieur comme à l'intérieur, l'accent a été mis sur la pureté des lignes. Les intérieurs blancs, aux sols de marbre grec blanc dans les parties publiques, semblent encore plus épurés grâce au recours à des plafonds suspendus qui dissimulent les systèmes de sécurité et les sources d'éclairage naturelles ou artificielles.

_Dieser Museumsbau mit einer Gesamtfläche von 7 000 m² steht auf einem dreieckigen Grundstück inmitten der Klosteranlage Santo Domingo de Bonaval aus dem 17. Jahrhundert. Mit ortstypischen Granitfassaden antwortet der Bau in einer modernen und zugleich sich respektvoll einfügenden Architektursprache auf seinen Kontext und harmonisiert mit den benachbarten historischen Gebäuden. »Ich kann es nicht genau erklären,« so Siza, »bin aber fest davon überzeugt – weil ich Santiago viele Male besucht habe –, daß sich der Neubau auf sehr natürliche Weise in diese Stadtlandschaft einpaßt.« Mit langgestreckten, zum größten Teil geschlossenen Fassaden geht der Architekt auf benachbarte Mauern aus roh behauenem Naturstein ein. Zum Zeitpunkt der Auftragserteilung gab es weder eine Sammlung noch einen Museumskurator, so daß Siza bei der Innengliederung eine flexible Nutzung einplanen mußte, die er in zwei sich überlappenden Bauvolumen auf je L-förmigem Grundriß umsetzte. Sowohl innen als auch außen legte Siza die Betonung auf eine Reinheit der Linienführung. Die weißen Interieurs mit Böden aus weißem griechischem Marmor in den öffentlichen Bereichen wirken noch klarer aufgrund der abgehängten Decken, die Sicherheitssysteme und Lichtquellen verdecken.

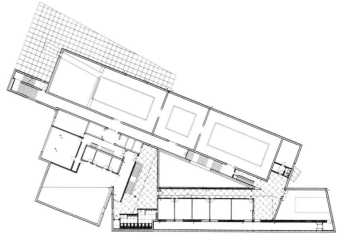

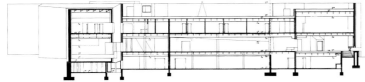

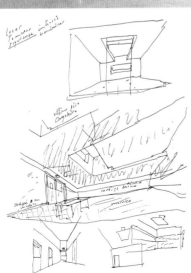

_Fires ravaged some eighteen buildings in the historic Chiado area of Lisbon in 1988. Although Álvaro Siza was given the mission of studying the renewal of this district, he agreed from the outset to one important condition: that the remaining walls of the damaged buildings be retained to the greatest extent possible. As a result, when one walks along the Rua Nova do Almada, where entrances to the Camara Chaves and Castro & Melo Buildings are located, it is not readily apparent that Siza has intervened here. Rather, it is within the structure, for example in the apartment of Henrique Chaves, that his style and presence can be felt. The volumes of the living space necessarily have some relation to what existed before the fire, if only because of the disposition of the windows, but here, as elsewhere, the architect has seen to every detail, down to the ashtrays. At once modern and somehow rather complex and mysterious, the spaces of Álvaro Siza blend with those of the old Chiado until no distinction can be perceived between the two.

_En 1988, un gigantesque incendie ravagea 18 immeubles du quartier historique de Chiado, à Lisbonne. En prenant en charge la mission d'étude de la rénovation de ce quartier, Álvaro Siza donne son accord dès le départ à une importante condition: conserver le maximum de façades et de murs subsistants. Aujourd'hui, en se promenant le long de la rue Nova do Almada où se situent les entrées des immeubles Camara Chaves et Castro & Melo, il ne semble pas évident que l'on se trouve face à des interventions de Siza. C'est plutôt à l'intérieur de ces structures, et par exemple dans l'appartement d'Henrique Chaves, que son style et sa présence se font sentir. Les volumes ont obligatoirement un certain rapport avec ce qui existait auparavant, ne serait-ce que par la disposition des fenêtres, mais là comme ailleurs, l'architecte s'est préoccupé du moindre détail, jusqu'aux cendriers. À la fois modernes et d'une certaine façon assez complexes et mystérieux, les espaces dessinés par Siza se fondent dans ceux du vieux Chiado sans que l'on ne puisse vraiment les distinguer les uns des autres.

_Im Jahr 1988 zerstörte ein Großfeuer 18 Gebäude im Chiado-Bezirk der Altstadt von Lissabon. Álvaro Siza wurde mit einer Studie zum Wiederaufbau dieses Bezirks beauftragt und erklärte sich von Anfang an mit einer wichtigen Bedingung einverstanden, nämlich die stehengebliebenen Außenmauern der beschädigten Häuser so weit wie möglich zu erhalten. Wenn man heute die Rua Nova do Almada entlanggeht, in der sich die Zugänge zu den Gebäuden Camara Chaves und Castro & Melo befinden, ist nicht auf den ersten Blick erkennbar, daß Siza hier eingegriffen hat. Erst im Innern, etwa in der Wohnung von Henrique Chaves, sind Sizas Stil und Wirken sichtbar. Natürlich beziehen sich die Dimensionen der Räume auf den früheren Altbau, und sei es nur durch die Plazierung der Fenster, aber auch hier hat der Architekt jedes Detail gestaltet – bis hin zu den Aschenbechern. Die von Álvaro Siza geschaffenen Räumlichkeiten sind modern und zugleich auf eine gewisse Weise komplex und geheimnisvoll. Sie fügen sich so nahtlos in den historischen Chiado ein, daß nicht zwischen Alt und Neu unterschieden werden kann.

Reconstruction Plan for the Chiado Area,
Lisbon, Portugal, 1988–
Camara Chaves Building, 1991–1996
Castro & Melo Building, 1991–1994
Baixa/Chiado Subway Station, 1992–1998

_Near the Chiado District, where he has rebuilt a number of buildings destroyed by fire, Álvaro Siza designed the vast **Baixa/Chiado Subway Station,** with its characteristic white tiles, some of which have a decor drawn by the artist Ângelo de Sousa.

_Près du quartier du Chiado, pour lequel il a reconstruit un certain nombre d'immeubles détruits par un incendie, Álvaro Siza a conçu la vaste **station de métro Baixa/Chiado,** aux carrelages blancs caractéristiques, dont certains sont décorés d'un motif dû à Ângelo de Sousa.

_In der Nähe des Stadtbezirks Chiado, wo Álvaro Siza eine Reihe von Gebäuden wieder aufbaute, die durch den großen Brand zerstört worden waren, entwarf er auch die weitläufige **Baixa/Chiado U-Bahnstation** mit ihren charakteristischen weißen Fliesen, von denen einige mit Ornamenten von Ângelo de Sousa verziert wurden.

_Behind facades of a burnt-out residential building, Álvaro Siza designed apartments that are inspired by the spirit of the original, without attempting to recreate pre-existing spaces. Here, in the apartment of the **Camara Chaves Building**'s promoter, Siza also designed the furniture. On the right hand page, drawings by the architect are reproduced on the white tiles in the entrance to the building.

_Derrière les façades conservées d'un immeuble résidentiel entièrement détruit par le feu, Álvaro Siza a conçu des appartements inspirés de ceux qui existaient à l'origine, sans pour autant recréer les mêmes espaces antérieurs. Ici, Siza a également dessiné le mobilier de l'appartement du promoteur Henrique Chaves **(immeuble Camara Chaves)**. À droite, des dessins de l'architecte sont reproduits sur les carrelages blancs de l'entrée de l'immeuble.

_Hinter den Fassaden der durch das Feuer zerstörten Mietwohnhäuser schuf Siza neue Wohnungen, zu deren Gestaltung er sich vom Original inspirieren ließ, ohne zu versuchen, die alten Räume exakt nachzubilden. Für die hier abgebildete Wohnung des Bauherrn des **Camara Chaves-Gebäudes** entwarf Siza auch die Möbel. Zeichnungen des Architekten sind auf den weißen Kacheln im Hauseingang reproduziert worden (rechte Seite).

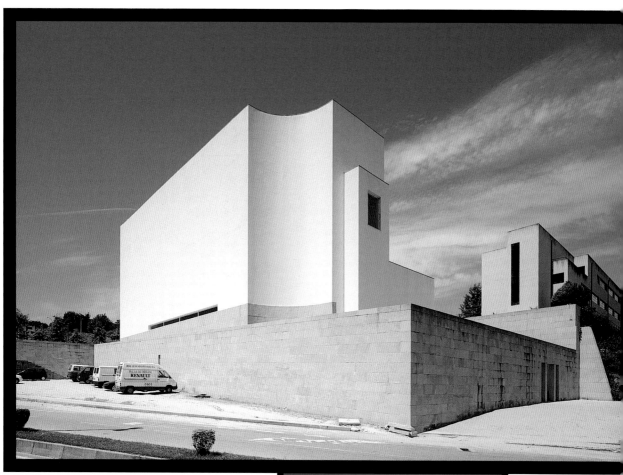

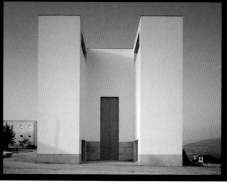

Santa Maria Church,
Marco de Canavezes, Portugal, 1990–1996

Parish Center,
Marco de Canavezes, Portugal, 2003–

_Designed in close collaboration with the parish priest, Father Nuno Higino, this spare, white church is one of Siza's purest and most powerful works. The simple, 30 meter long nave has twin 10 meter high doors, which open out onto the future square where the Parish Center is to be built when the church raises sufficient funds. Within the church, Siza has taken great care in the design of numerous details, ranging from the chairs to the altar and even to the gilt wood cross, which stands to the right of the altar as the priest faces the congregation. Local construction techniques were used to reduce costs, but Siza's touch is visible at every point, particularly in the very successful "light chimneys," which bring two bands of light down behind the altar, suggesting the presence of a cross without actually drawing it out. These light wells will also serve the funerary chapel located directly below the altar. Unusual features such as the tile-clad baptistery area located immediately to the left of the main entrance, and the low strip window that offers the 400 seated parishioners a view of neighboring mountains, ensure that this church is full of surprises, despite its apparent austerity.

_Dessinée en étroite collaboration avec le prêtre de la paroisse, le père Nuno Higino, cette austère église blanche est l'une des œuvres les plus pures et les plus marquantes de Siza. Au bout de la simple nef de 30 mètres de long, deux portes hautes de 10 mètres ouvrent sur une future place qui accueillera le centre paroissial lorsque l'église aura trouvé les financements nécessaires. À l'intérieur, Siza a dessiné avec le plus grand soin de nombreux détails, des chaises à l'autel et jusqu'à la croix de bois doré, dressée à gauche de celui-ci. Les techniques locales de construction ont permis de réduire les coûts, mais la présence de l'architecte reste partout visible, en particulier dans les «cheminées de lumière» très réussies qui créent deux bandeaux lumineux derrière l'autel pour suggérer la présence d'une croix. Ces puits de lumière éclairent également la chapelle funéraire, située directement sous l'autel. Le baptistère couvert de carrelage à gauche de l'entrée principale est inhabituel, ainsi que la longue fenêtre en bandeau qui offre aux 400 fidèles une vue sur les montagnes avoisinantes. Malgré son austérité apparente, cette église révèle bien des surprises.

_Dieser schlichte weiße Kirchenbau entstand in enger Zusammenarbeit zwischen dem Architekten und dem Gemeindepfarrer, Pater Nuno Higino, und gehört zu Sizas klarsten und ausdrucksstärksten Gebäuden. Vom Vorplatz, auf dem später das Pfarrzentrum entstehen soll, gelangt man durch ein 10 Meter hohes Doppelportal in den 30 Meter langen Kirchenraum. Siza hat mit großer Sorgfalt eine Fülle von Ausstattungselementen entworfen: von der Bestuhlung und dem Altar bis zum vergoldeten Holzkreuz, das links neben dem Altar auf dem Boden steht. Traditionelle Bautechniken wurden angewendet, um die Kosten zu reduzieren, aber Sizas Wirken ist überall sichtbar, besonders in den gelungenen »Lichtkaminen«, durch die Tageslicht die Wand hinter dem Altar hinabflutet und ein Kreuz angedeutet wird. Diese Lichtschächte lassen das Tageslicht auch in die unter dem Altar befindliche Grabkapelle einfallen. Ungewöhnliche Elemente wie die mit Fliesen verkleidete Taufkapelle links neben dem Hauptportal oder das tiefliegende Fenster, das den sitzenden Gemeindemitgliedern einen Ausblick auf die nahegelegenen Berge bietet, schaffen einen Kirchenbau, der trotz seiner offensichtlichen Schlichtheit voller Überraschungen steckt.

Vitra International Office Furniture Factory,
Weil am Rhein, Germany, 1991–1994

_The Vitra Factory is located close to the Swiss border, near Basle. It is the site of numerous buildings designed by well-known architects such as Nicholas Grimshaw, Frank O. Gehry, Tadao Ando, and Zaha Hadid. With a surface area of 11,600 square meters, Álvaro Siza's factory is the largest building on the site. With its monumental, windowless Dutch brick facade and Portuguese granite base, this building stands out from the neighboring structures. Though it does seem to be a distant echo of much older factory designs, Siza's building has an austerity that is in marked contrast to the "deconstructivist" exuberance of Hadid's small concrete fire station, which stands just next to it, or to Gehry's nearby sculptural white plaster museum. Within the factory, Siza again looks in an unexpected direction, creating two building-like outposts, one for the office of the superintendent, and the other a technical control station set up on four columns. Siza's Vitra Factory gives the impression that he chose to react to his prestigious architectural neighbors by pushing his normal penchant for austerity to its limit. This exterior austerity is relieved only by an unusual arched bridge, linking the building to Nicholas Grimshaw's earlier metal structure.

_L'usine Vitra se trouve à proximité de la frontière suisse, près de Bâle. Sur son vaste terrain s'élèvent plusieurs bâtiments dus à des architectes célèbres, dont Nicholas Grimshaw, Frank O. Gehry, Tadao Ando et Zaha Hadid. Avec ses 11 600 m², l'usine construite par Siza est le plus vaste de tous. Sa façade monumentale sans fenêtre, plaquée de briques hollandaises, et sa base en granit portugais la singularisent par rapport aux constructions qui l'entourent. Bien qu'elle fasse penser à un lointain écho de modèles d'usines bien plus anciennes, cette réalisation présente une austérité en contraste marqué avec l'exubérance déconstructiviste du petit poste de secours des pompiers de Hadid – juste à côté –, ou des façades à l'enduit blanc du proche et très sculptural musée de Gehry. À l'intérieur, Siza nous entraîne une fois encore dans une direction inattendue, créant deux avant-postes qui sont presque des bâtiments en soi, l'un pour le bureau du directeur et l'autre un poste de contrôle technique élevé sur quatre colonnes. L'usine Vitra donne ainsi l'impression que l'architecte a choisi de réagir à ses prestigieux voisins architecturaux en poussant ses penchants naturels à l'austérité jusqu'à leurs limites. La rigueur de l'extérieur n'est rompue que par une curieuse passerelle en arc qui relie le bâtiment à celui, métallique et antérieur, de Nicholas Grimshaw.

_Das Fabrikgelände der Firma Vitra befindet sich in der Nähe der Schweizer Grenze und der Stadt Basel. Mehrere international bekannte Architekten haben je ein Gebäude des Ensembles entworfen: Nicholas Grimshaw, Frank O. Gehry, Tadao Ando und Zaha Hadid. Mit einer Gesamtfläche von 11 600 m² ist Sizas neue Produktionshalle das größte Gebäude auf dem Fabrikgelände und hebt sich mit ihrer monumentalen geschlossenen Fassade aus holländischem Klinker mit Sockel aus portugiesischem Granit deutlich von den anderen Bauten ab. Der Neubau wirkt zwar in gewisser Hinsicht wie ein Echo auf viel ältere Industriebauten, steht aber aufgrund seiner Reduziertheit hier im krassen Gegensatz zum »dekonstruktivistischen« Überschwang von Hadids kleiner Feuerwache aus Beton direkt neben Sizas Halle und zu Gehrys plastisch geformtem, weiß verputztem Vitra Design Museum. Im Innern der Fabrikhalle ist Siza wieder einmal ungewöhnliche Wege gegangen, indem er zwei Konstruktionen einfügte: einen Baukörper für die Räume der Produktionsleitung und einen auf vier Stützen ruhenden zentralen Bau für die Steuerungstechnik. Sizas Produktionshalle für Vitra erweckt den Eindruck, als habe der Architekt ganz bewußt – als Reaktion auf die ausgefallenen Nachbarbauten seiner berühmten Kollegen – seine Vorliebe für das Schlichte auf die Spitze getrieben. Die äußere formale Strenge wird nur unterbrochen von einer ungewöhnlichen Bogenbrücke, die die neue Produktionshalle mit Nicholas Grimshaws wellblechverkleidetem Fabrikbau verbindet.

_Situated next to Zaha Hadid's Fire Station, Álvaro Siza's Factory building is intentionally austere. Its brick facing also contrasts with the concrete chosen by Hadid.

_Près du poste de pompiers dessiné par Zaha Hadid, l'usine d'Álvaro Siza est d'un style volontairement austère. Son parement de brique contraste avec le béton choisi par Zaha Hadid.

_Neben Zaha Hadids Feuerwache nimmt sich Álvaro Sizas Fabrikhalle bewußt karg und streng aus. Auch ihre Ziegelmauerwerksfassade kontrastiert mit dem Sichtbeton der Feuerwache.

Álvaro Siza Office,
Porto, Portugal, 1993–1997

_Located relatively close to Siza's Porto Faculty of Architecture, just above the Douro River estuary, this five-story U-shaped office building houses not only his offices, but also those of Fernando Távora, Rogerio Cavaca, and Eduardo Souto de Moura (above), as well as a group of engineers. The architects are lodged in descending order of age, with Távora on the top level and Siza below him. Although Siza drew up the plans for this building in agreement with his colleagues, its concrete structure and interior details such as linoleum floors do not give the whole an appearance of the sort of careful detailing typical of his designs. Features such as lights, hand railing, or door handles by Siza are, however, present here, and the nature of the detailing is naturally related to cost considerations. Flexible in its open floor plan, the building almost entirely occupies its 3,000 square meter site, making it an unexpected, if not awkward, presence in an area of more traditional private residences.

_Situé relativement près de la faculté d'architecture édifiée par Siza, juste au-dessus de l'estuaire du Douro, cet immeuble de bureaux en forme de «U», de cinq étages de haut, abrite son agence, et celle de Fernando Távora, Rogerio Cavaca et Eduardo Souto de Moura (ci-dessus), ainsi qu'un groupe d'ingénieurs. Les architectes sont logés par ordre d'âge descendant, Távora au sommet, et Siza juste en dessous. Bien que Siza ait dessiné les plans de cet immeuble en accord avec ses collègues, sa structure en béton et certains détails intérieurs, comme les sols en linoléum, ne donnent pas à l'ensemble l'apparence soignée typique de ses projets habituels. Cependant, on retrouve des éléments comme les luminaires, la rampe ou les poignées de porte, et l'on peut penser que le degré d'exécution a été lié à des considérations de coût. De plan ouvert, donc souple, l'immeuble occupe presque entièrement les 3 000 m² de son terrain, ce qui lui donne un aspect inattendu, à la limite de la maladresse, dans un environnement de résidences privées plus traditionnelles.

_Nicht weit von seiner Alma Mater, der Architekturfakultät der Universität Porto, hat Siza oberhalb der Douro-Mündung ein fünfgeschossiges, U-förmiges Bürohaus gebaut, in dem sich nicht nur sein eigenes Architekturbüro, sondern auch die Büros von Fernando Távora, Rogerio Cavaca, Eduardo Souto de Moura (oben) und einer Gruppe von Ingenieuren befinden. Die Architekten sind in der Abfolge ihres Alters (von oben nach unten) untergebracht, mit Távora im obersten Geschoß und Siza unter ihm. Siza hat diesen Betonbau in Abstimmung mit seinen Kollegen erstellt, aber die ganze Erscheinung und Innenausstattung des Gebäudes, zu der auch Linoleumböden gehören, weisen nicht die für die anderen Werke Sizas so typische Sorgfalt im Detail auf. Dennoch gibt es auch hier die von Siza selbst entworfenen Lampen, Handläufe oder Türgriffe, aber die Ausstattungsdetails sind natürlich von Kostenerwägungen geprägt. Das Gebäude besitzt flexible, offene Grundrisse und überbaut fast das gesamte 3 000 m² große Grundstück. Das macht es zu einem ungewöhnlichen, wenn nicht sogar etwas unangenehmen »Nachbarn« in einem Wohngebiet mit traditioneller Wohnhausarchitektur.

Vieira de Castro House,
Famalicão, Portugal, 1984–1998

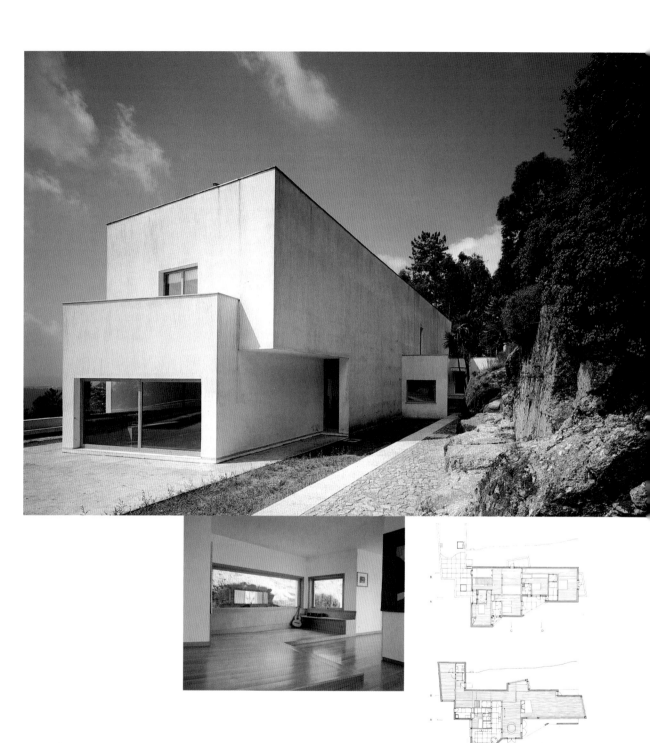

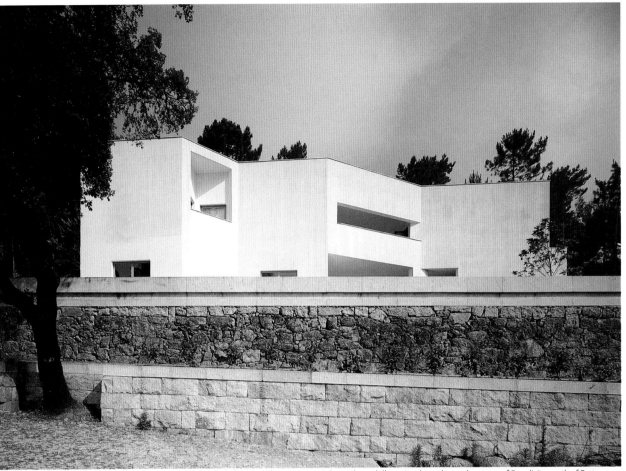

_More than fourteen years in the making, this house, built for a local businessman, is located on a hilltop site above the modern town of Famalicão, north of Porto.
It is approached by a forest path, and the visitor first encounters sculptural Corten steel entry gates. Like the rusticated stone walls that define the terraces of the residence, these gates are the work of Siza. The visitor is led along a path that threads between the rectangular outdoor swimming pool and an existing rock outcropping to the discreet main door. Once indoors, a gently sloping, slightly curved wooden passage leads down to the living room, with its numerous views out onto the neighboring, mountainous countryside. The chimney, the living and dining room furniture, the kitchen fixtures – everything is designed by Siza. Obviously committed to a lengthy and complex process, the owners of the house wait patiently for the last pieces of furniture to arrive. Although this clearly is a house for wealthy clients, a modern discretion bordering on austerity is the rule in this light-filled residence.

_Il a fallu plus de 14 années pour édifier cette maison, construite pour un homme d'affaires local au sommet d'une colline qui domine la ville moderne de Famalicão, au nord de Porto. Le visiteur y accède par un chemin forestier et se trouve dans un premier temps face à un portail d'entrée sculptural en acier Corten, œuvre de Siza, de même que les murs en pierre rustiquée qui délimitent les terrasses de la résidence. Il emprunte ensuite un chemin qui se glisse entre la piscine extérieure rectangulaire et une excroissance rocheuse pour se rendre à la discrète porte principale. Une fois à l'intérieur, un cheminement parqueté descend selon une courbe légère vers la salle de séjour aux multiples ouvertures sur le voisinage et le paysage montagneux. La cheminée, le mobilier du séjour et de la salle à manger, les équipements de la cuisine, ont tous été dessinés par Siza. Conscients d'être plongés dans un processus long et complexe, les propriétaires ont patiemment attendu que les derniers meubles arrivent. Bien qu'il s'agisse d'une résidence pour clients aisés, une discrétion moderne qui frise l'austérité est de règle dans cette résidence baignée de lumière.

_Der Bau dieses Einfamilienhauses für einen ortsansässigen Geschäftsmann nahm 14 Jahre in Anspruch. Das Haus steht auf einer Anhöhe oberhalb der modernen Stadt Famalicão nördlich von Porto. Man nähert sich dem Haus über eine schmale Waldstraße, und dem Besucher bietet sich als erstes der Anblick eines plastisch geformten Zufahrtstors aus Corten-Stahl. Wie die unbehauenen Natursteinmauern, die die Terrassen des Wohnhauses einfassen, ist auch das Tor von Siza entworfen worden. Der Besucher wird einen Weg entlanggeführt, der sich zwischen dem rechteckigen Schwimmbecken und einer natürlichen Felsformation bis zur etwas versteckten Eingangstür des Hauses hinzieht. Innen gelangt man über einen leicht abfallenden Holzkorridor hinunter ins Wohnzimmer, von dem aus man viele schöne Ausblicke auf das bergige Umland hat. Der Kamin, die Möbel für Wohn- und Eßzimmer, die Kücheneinrichtung – alles hat Siza entworfen. Die Besitzer haben sich offenbar ganz bewußt auf den langwierigen und komplizierten Entstehungsprozeß ihres Hauses eingestellt und warten geduldig auf die Lieferung der letzten noch fehlenden Möbelstücke. Obwohl es sich hier ganz offensichtlich um das Haus wohlhabender Leute handelt, erscheinen die lichtdurchfluteten modernen Räume zurückhaltend, fast karg.

Portuguese Pavilion, Expo '98,
Lisbon, Portugal, 1995–1998

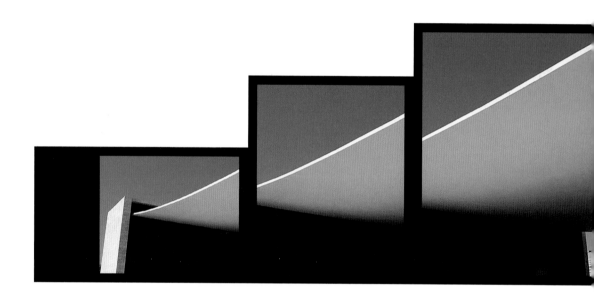

_Built on the shores of the Tagus, the Portuguese Pavilion occupies an axial site, not far from the main entrance to Expo '98. As opposed to many of the surrounding buildings, Siza chose a discreet, horizontal design. His brief included a large outside space for ceremonial functions. He met this requirement with an unusual curved concrete "veil," which is suspended at either end from steel cables. Red and green ceramic cladding is used at either end of this outdoor space, marking one of Siza's first exterior uses of a traditional Portuguese building material. The main structure, which will serve in the future as the seat of the Portuguese Council of Ministers, is designed for maximum flexibility. The large, high-ceilinged rooms on the ground floor are used for the Expo '98 multimedia presentation, in spaces designed by Eduardo Souto de Moura. On the upper level around a central courtyard, the so-called "VIP" rooms are entirely designed and decorated by Siza.

_Édifié sur une rive du Tage, le Pavillon du Portugal occupe un site axial non loin de l'entrée principale de l'Expo '98. À l'encontre de beaucoup des bâtiments environnants, Siza a imaginé un projet discret de lignes horizontales. Le cahier des charges demandant un vaste espace extérieur pour les cérémonies, il a imaginé un étonnant «voile» de béton incurvé, suspendu à ses deux extrémités par des câbles d'acier. De chaque côté du bâtiment, un parement en carreaux de céramique rouges et verts est la première utilisation extérieure par Siza de ce matériau typiquement portugais. La structure principale, qui servira de siège au Conseil des ministres, a été conçue pour permettre le maximum de souplesse. Les vastes salles à haut plafond du rez-de-chaussée ont été occupées par les présentations multimédias de l'Expo '98, dans des espaces dessinés par Eduardo Souto de Moura. Au niveau supérieur, autour d'une cour centrale, les salles "VIP" ont été entièrement conçues et décorées par Siza.

_Der Portugiesische Pavillon steht auf einem axialen Gelände in der Nähe des Haupteingangs des Expo-Geländes am Ufer des Tagus. Im Gegensatz zu den Architekten vieler umliegender Pavillons entschied sich Siza für eine unaufdringliche, horizontale Bauform. Die Ausschreibung forderte einen großen Freiplatz für offizielle Anlässe. Siza löste die Aufgabe mit einem ungewöhnlichen geschwungenen »Segel« aus Beton, das an beiden Enden mittels Stahlkabeln aufgehängt ist. Rote und grüne Keramikfliesen zieren beide Seiten des Freiplatzes, ein traditionelles portugiesisches Baumaterial, das Siza hier zum ersten Mal im Außenbau einsetzt. Der Hauptbau, der in Zukunft als Sitz des portugiesischen Ministerrats dienen wird, ist auf größtmögliche räumliche Flexibilität angelegt. Die großen, hohen Räume im Erdgeschoß wurden während der Expo '98 für die Multi-Media-Ausstellung genutzt; sie sind von Eduardo Souto de Moura ausgestaltet worden. Im Obergeschoß befinden sich um einen zentralen Innenhof die sogenannten VIP-Räume, deren Innenausbau und Einrichtungen Siza entworfen hat.

_The exhibition areas in the Portuguese Pavilion were designed by Eduardo Souto de Moura in collaboration with Álvaro Siza.

_Les espaces d'exposition du Pavillon du Portugal ont été conçus par Eduardo Souto de Moura en collaboration avec Álvaro Siza.

_Die Ausstellungsbereiche im Portugiesischen Pavillon wurden von Eduardo Souto de Moura in Zusammenarbeit mit Álvaro Siza entworfen.

_The drawings reproduced on the walls of the VIP reception areas as well as the furniture are by Álvaro Siza.

_Les dessins figurant sur les murs des espaces de réception réservés aux personnalités, ainsi que le mobilier, sont d'Álvaro Siza.

_Die Zeichnungen für die Wanddekorationen in den VIP-Empfangsräumen und die Möbelentwürfe stammen von Álvaro Siza.

Rectory of the University of Alicante,
Alicante, Spain, 1995–1998

_Built on the site of the former Rabasa military airport, whose former control tower has been conserved, the Rectory of the University of Alicante is "thought of as a closed fortress defending itself, in the Hispanic-Muslim manner, from the hot climate, accentuating the distinctly planar character of the campus," according to Siza's project description. Shaped like the letter "H," the building is for the most part set out on two levels, with classrooms, an auditorium, and a semicircular "grand hall" on the ground floor, as well as spaces for the Law and Linguistics departments and the Office of International Relations. Offices on the second floor are laid out above their respective departments. The stone floors seen on the ground floor are replaced by wooden ones on the upper level. The exterior finish is "a stucco mixed with pulverized brick complemented by a 1.80 meter high stone base."

_Sur le site de l'ancien aérodrome militaire de Rabasa, dont la tour de contrôle a été conservée, ce rectorat a été «pensé comme une forteresse se défendant à la manière hispano-mauresque contre la chaleur du climat en accentuant le caractère plat du campus», selon la description que donne Siza de son projet. En forme de «H», le bâtiment s'organise pour sa plus grande partie sur deux niveaux. Le rez-de-chaussée est occupé par des salles de cours, un auditorium, un grand hall semi-circulaire, ainsi que des espaces pour les départements de droit et de linguistique et le bureau des relations internationales. Les bureaux de l'étage sont implantés au-dessus des départements auxquels ils sont rattachés. Les sols sont en pierre au rez-de-chaussée et en bois à l'étage. Les façades sont recouvertes d'un «enduit mélangé à de la brique pulvérisée, appliqué au-dessus d'une base en pierre de 1,80 mètre de haut».

_Das Dekanatsgebäude der Universität Alicante entstand auf dem Gelände des ehemaligen Militärflughafens Rabasa, dessen Kontrollturm erhalten blieb, und ist konzipiert als »geschlossene Festung, die sich in spanisch-maurischer Tradition gegen das heiße Klima verteidigt und den deutlich flach ausgebreiteten Charakter der Universitäts-anlage betont«, so Siza in seiner Projektbeschreibung. Das in weiten Teilen zweigeschossige, H-förmige Gebäude enthält Unterrichtsräume, einen großen Hörsaal und eine halbkreisförmige »Große Halle« im Erdgeschoß, außerdem die Räume der Jura- und Linguistikfakultäten und die Büros für internationale Beziehungen. Die Büros im Obergeschoß gehören zu den jeweils darunterliegenden Abteilungen. Die Räumlichkeiten im Erdgeschoß haben Steinfußböden, in der oberen Etage Holzböden. Die Fassaden sind »verputzt mit einem Gemisch aus Putzmörtel und zerstoßenen Ziegelsteinen; der 1,80 Meter hohe Sockel besteht aus Natursteinen«.

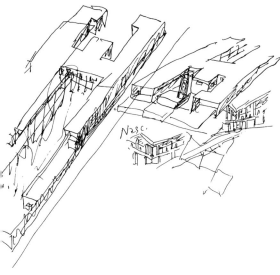

Boavista Building,
Porto, Portugal, 1991–1998

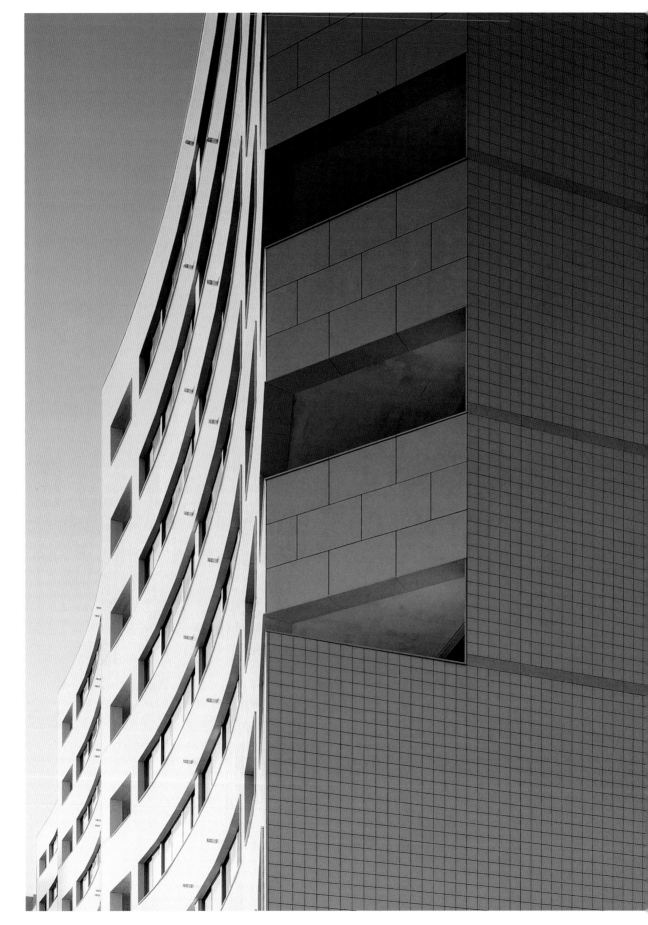

_This large, rather luxurious residential building was originally intended to be the first of a series of similar structures, in an area of Porto that already includes numerous high-rise apartment buildings. Disagreements with the promoter led to the construction of a single building clad entirely in white tiles, a first for Álvaro Siza. Although it appears from a distance to be rather monotonous, the building is in fact quite subtle and varied in its surface effects. The large, comfortable apartments include a limited number of details designed by Siza, but cost constraints in such a large building must inevitably lead to the use of standardized materials. Álvaro Siza seems to harbor a certain frustration over this project, perhaps because the planned series of structures could not be built, but it is not obvious that his talents are in fact well suited to such large-scale repetitive high-rise buildings.

_À l'origine, ce grand immeuble d'appartements assez luxueux devait être le premier d'une série de bâtiments similaires, dans un quartier de Porto qui compte déjà de nombreux immeubles résidentiels de grande hauteur. Des désaccords avec le promoteur ont réduit le programme à un seul immeuble entièrement revêtu de carrelage blanc, une première pour Álvaro Siza. S'il semble assez monotone vu de loin, le Boa Vista offre en fait un jeu d'effets de surface assez subtil et varié. Dans les vastes et confortables appartements, les interventions de Siza sur les détails sont peu nombreuses, les contraintes de coûts de ce type de réalisation ayant inévitablement poussé au choix de matériaux standardisés. Álvaro Siza semble témoigner d'une certaine frustration sur ce projet, peut-être parce que les autres immeubles prévus n'ont pu être réalisés, mais aussi parce qu'il n'est pas évident que son talent soit réellement adapté à ce type de grands immeubles répétitifs.

_Dieses große, ziemlich luxuriöse Mietwohnhaus sollte ursprünglich das erste einer Reihe ähnlicher Gebäude in einem Bezirk von Porto sein, in dem bereits zahlreiche hohe Wohnblöcke stehen. Unstimmigkeiten mit dem Bauträger führten jedoch dazu, daß nur ein einziges der geplanten Häuser gebaut wurde. Es ist als erstes von allen Bauten Sizas völlig mit weißen Fliesen verkleidet. Obwohl es aus der Entfernung eher monoton erscheint, bietet der Komplex bei näherer Betrachtung doch sehr subtil variierende Oberflächen. Einige wenige Details der großen komfortablen Wohnungen sind auch hier von Siza gestaltet worden, ansonsten mußte er bei der Innenausstattung aus Kostengründen weitgehend mit Standardmaterialien arbeiten. Dieses Projekt hat bei Álvaro Siza offenbar eine gewisse Frustration hinterlassen, vielleicht weil er nicht alle geplanten Gebäude der Gesamtanlage realisieren konnte. Auf den ersten Blick ist jedenfalls nicht ersichtlich, daß sein Architekturstil und -talent für die Gestaltung eines so großen modularen Hochhauskomplexes tatsächlich geeignet ist.

Serralves Foundation,
Porto, Portugal, 1996–1999

_The Serralves Foundation was created through a unique partnership between the Portuguese government and fifty private sector partners. Established in the Quinta de Serralves, a large property including a main house built in the 1930s for the Count of Vizela, which is located close to the center of Porto, the Foundation specializes in contemporary art. Siza's new structure, located in the park of the Foundation, is both substantial in size and ambitious in scope. Using a suspended ceiling system similar to the one he devised for the Galician Center for Contemporary Art, Siza designed a number of large, flexible galleries, intended not for a permanent collection but exclusively for temporary shows. Internal courtyards and numerous windows permit the visitor to remain in contact with the very attractive park environment (3 hectares of which Siza is responsible for), while the interior provides all of the facilities that are now expected of modern museums, including a gift shop, cafeteria, and an auditorium. The whole is built with a visible attention to detail, which is typical of Siza, but here he has been given the means to carry out his ideas.

_La Fondation Serralves a été créée grâce à une association originale entre le gouvernement portugais et 50 partenaires du secteur privé. Installée dans la Quinta de Serralves, un vaste domaine comprenant une résidence construite dans les années 30 pour le comte de Vizela, situé non loin du centre de Porto, la Fondation se consacre à l'art contemporain. La nouvelle construction due à Siza, dans le parc même de la Fondation, est importante à la fois par sa taille et ses ambitions. Siza a conçu un certain nombre de grandes galeries souples destinées non pas à une collection permanente, mais à des expositions temporaires. Elles sont équipées du même type de plafond suspendu utilisé pour le Centre galicien d'art contemporain. Des cours intérieures et de nombreuses fenêtres permettent au visiteur de rester en contact avec le superbe parc de 3 hectares dont l'architecte est également responsable. L'intérieur offre tous les équipements que l'on peut attendre d'un musée moderne, dont une boutique de cadeaux, une cafétéria et un auditorium. L'ensemble est construit avec un amour du détail, typique de Siza, qui a enfin disposé de moyens financiers adaptés à la mise en œuvre de ses idées.

_Die Serralves-Stiftung ist aus einer einzigartigen Zusammenarbeit der portugiesischen Regierung mit 50 Partnern aus der Privatwirtschaft entstanden. Die Stiftung fördert zeitgenössische Kunst und hat ihr Domizil in der Quinta de Serralves, einem weitläufigen Anwesen unweit des Stadtzentrums von Porto, mit einer Villa, die in den 30er Jahren für den Grafen von Vizela errichtet wurde. Sizas Neubau im Park der Stiftung ist ein großangelegtes, ehrgeiziges Projekt. Siza schuf große, flexibel zu nutzende Galerien mit abgehängten Deckenkonstruktionen, ähnlich wie im Galicischen Museum für Zeitgenössische Kunst in Santiago de Compostela. Die Galerien beherbergen keine ständige Sammlung, sondern sind ausschließlich für Wechselausstellungen bestimmt. Innenhöfe und zahlreiche Fensteröffnungen ermöglichen dem Besucher Blickkontakt zum umliegenden Park (3 Hektar der Parkfläche wurden von Siza gestaltet). Im Inneren sind alle Einrichtungen vorhanden, die man heute in einem modernen Museum erwartet: ein Museumsshop, eine Cafeteria und ein Vortragssaal. Die Gesamtanlage läßt die für Siza typische Detailsorgfalt erkennen, und hier standen ihm die Mittel zur Verfügung, um seine Ideen auch ausführen zu können.

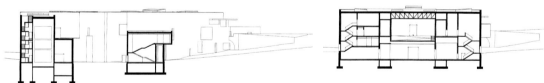

_Siza is a master of the subtle manipulation of light and materials, here to the benefit of the art works that are placed in spaces whose architecture and lighting can be modified to accommodate specific types of installation.

_Siza est un des maîtres de la manipulation subtile de la lumière et des matériaux, ici au bénéfice d'œuvres d'art disposées dans des espaces dont l'architecture et l'éclairage peuvent être modifiés selon les types de présentation.

_Siza ist ein Meister der subtilen Gestaltung mit Licht und Material. Im Vordergrund stehen dabei die Kunstwerke, die in Räumen präsentiert werden, deren Innenausstattung und Lichtdesign je nach Art der Ausstellung verändert werden können.

Santo Ovidio Estate, Douro Litoral,
Portugal, 1989–1992; 1997–2001

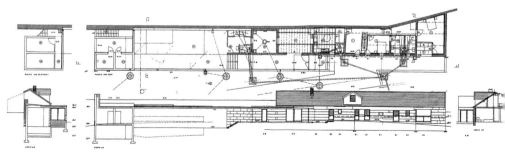

_Formerly at the center of a large farm, this house is now located on a three hectare site. The project consisted in renovating the 600 square meter main house, adding a 520 square meter covered swimming pool and annex, as well as building a small (44 square meter) chapel. A wall surrounds the house and a vineyard, and a baroque fountain attached to the wall defines the inner area. Since the original house had no internal staircase linking the upper and ground floors, Siza added one at the point where the library is now located on the higher level. Also situated on this floor are a living room, a dining room and a kitchen, while the ground floor now houses another living room, a game room and three bedrooms. Reusing part of the farm walls, the architect created the flat-roofed pool area using zinc and granite for the exterior cladding, and marble, wood and tiles inside. As has often been the case in his other projects, Alvaro Siza discreetly renovated the gardens and belvedere to give this entire estate a modern unity that does not deny its more utilitarian past.

_Jadis située au centre d'un grand domaine agricole, cette maison se trouve aujourd'hui sur un terrain de trois hectares. Le programme consistait en la rénovation de la maison principale de 600 m², l'adjonction (520 m²) d'une piscine couverte, d'une annexe et d'une petite chapelle privée de 44 m². Un mur entoure la maison et une vigne tandis qu'une fontaine baroque murale annonce la zone privée. Comme la maison d'origine ne possédait pas d'escalier reliant le rez-de-chaussée et l'étage par l'intérieur, Siza dut en créer un dans ce qui est actuellement la bibliothèque, à l'étage. Sur le même niveau se trouvent un séjour, une salle à manger et une cuisine, tandis que le rez-de-chaussée comprend une autre salle à manger, une salle de jeux et trois chambres. C'est en réutilisant une partie des murs de la ferme ancienne que l'architecte a créé le volume à toit plat de la piscine, habillant l'extérieur de zinc et de granit, l'intérieur de marbre, de bois et de carrelage. Comme dans beaucoup de ses autres projets, il a discrètement rénové les jardins et le belvédère pour conférer à ce domaine une unité d'esprit contemporaine qui ne rejette pas son passé plus utilitaire.

_Früher bildete dieses Haus den Mittelpunkt eines großen Bauernhofes, heute steht es auf einem drei Hektar großen Gelände. Die Bauaufgabe bestand in der Restaurierung des Haupthauses mit einer Gesamtfläche von 600 m² und der Erweiterung um 520 m², einschließlich eines Hallenbades, sowie der Errichtung einer kleinen Kapelle (44 m²). Eine Mauer umgibt das Haus und einen Weinberg, und ein in die Wand integrierter barocker Brunnen akzentuiert den Hof. Da das alte Haus keine Innentreppe zwischen Erdgeschoß und oberem Stockwerk besaß, baute Siza eine an der Stelle ein, an der sich heute im Obergeschoß die Bibliothek befindet. Hier befinden sich auch ein Wohnzimmer, das Eßzimmer und die Küche; im Erdgeschoß sind ein weiterer Wohnraum, ein Spiel- und drei Schlafzimmer untergebracht. Unter Nutzung einiger stehengebliebener Mauern der alten Hofgebäude baute der Architekt die Schwimmhalle mit Flachdach, für die er außen Zinkblech und Granit und innen Marmor, Holz und Fliesen verwendete. Wie schon häufig bei seinen anderen Projekten überarbeitete Alvaro Siza auch hier die Gärten mitsamt dem Belvedere behutsam, um diesem ländlichen Anwesen eine moderne Geschlossenheit zu geben, ohne seine frühere landwirtschaftliche Nutzung zu verleugnen.

Van Middelem-Dupont House,
Oudenburg, Belgium, 1997–2001

_Here, too, Alvaro Siza engaged in the renovation of an existing farm and its conversion into a living space (with an art gallery). Three volumes are arranged in a U-shape around a patio, but Siza has taken care to distinguish the new from the old. He has used blue hard stone, western red cedar and a lead-covered roof in the 360 square meter extension, contrasting with the 1,414 square meter masonry and tile renovation. As Siza's statement on this project has it, "identifying with the history of interior and landscape paintings such as the Flemish primitives, well-proportioned openings toward the landscape bring a studied light into the interior". Indeed, both the interiors and Siza's taste for a rather complex modernity reflect his own style as much as they do Flemish art, but the exterior does make a concerted effort to create a harmony with local architecture. He speaks too of "unpretentious volumes", a point about which few would disagree. There is a subtle harmony between the new and the old that confirms Alvaro Siza's modesty and his very personal approach to the connection between old and new.

_Ici également, Alvaro Siza s'est engagé dans la rénovation d'une ferme existante pour la transformer en habitation et galerie d'art. Les trois volumes sont disposés en U autour d'un patio, mais Siza a pris soin de distinguer l'ancien du neuf. Il a utilisé une pierre bleue, le cèdre rouge et le plomb (pour le toit) pour l'extension de 360 m², qui contrastent avec les 1 414 m² de maçonnerie et de tuiles de la partie rénovée. Il a expliqué lui-même sa démarche: «En évocation de l'histoire de la peinture d'intérieurs et de paysages comme celle des primitifs flamands, des ouvertures bien proportionnées donnent sur le paysage pour apporter une lumière étudiée à l'intérieur.» Celui-ci reflète autant le goût de l'architecte pour une modernité complexe que l'art flamand, mais l'extérieur représente un effort concerté de retrouver une harmonie avec l'architecture locale. Siza parle également de «volumes sans prétention», point avec lequel on ne peut qu'agréer. On observe aussi une subtile harmonie entre le nouveau et l'ancien qui confirme la modestie d'approche de Siza dans ce domaine de la rénovation.

_Auch bei dieser Bauaufgabe handelte es sich um die Restaurierung eines alten Bauerngehöfts und dessen Umbau zu einem Wohnhaus (inklusive Kunstgalerie). Drei Baukörper umgeben heute U-förmig einen Hof, wobei Siza darauf achtete, den Neubau vom Altbau abzusetzen. Für den 360 m² großen, mit Blei gedeckten Anbau verwendete er bläuliche Natursteine und Zypressenholz als Kontrast zum restaurierten ziegelgedeckten, aus Stein gemauerten, 1 414 m² umfassenden Altbau. In Sizas Erläuterungstext heißt es: »In Übereinstimmung mit der Geschichte der Interieur- und Landschaftsmalerei etwa der flämischen Primitiven lassen gut proportionierte Öffnungen zur Landschaft mit Bedacht gesteuertes Licht in die Innenräume.« Dies reflektiert ebenso Sizas Vorliebe für eine relativ vielgestaltige Moderne wie die flämische Kunst. Aber das äußere Erscheinungsbild belegt sein Bemühen um Einklang mit der lokalen Architektur. Siza spricht auch von »unprätentiösen Volumen« und dem würden wohl nur Wenige widersprechen. Die subtile Harmonie zwischen Bestand und Anbau bestätigt Alvaro Sizas Bescheidenheit und den für ihn typischen Ansatz bei der Verbindung von Alt und Neu.

Chronological list of works

Pico do Areeiro Restaurant,
Madeira Island, Portugal, 1975 (design)

Largo da Lada Urban Rehabilitation,
Porto, Portugal, 1976 (design)

António Carlos Siza House,
Santo Tirso, Portugal, 1976–78

Quinta da Malagueira Social Housing,
Évora, Portugal, 1977–95

Hotel at Monte Picoto, Braga,
Portugal, 1978 (design, competition)

Borges & Irmão Bank,
Vila do Conde, Portugal, 1978–86

Maria Margarida House, Arcozelo,
Portugal, 1979–87

Goerlitzer Bad (swimming pool),
Berlin, Germany, 1979 (design)

Housing at Fraenkelufer, Berlin,
Germany, 1979 (design)

> 1980-89 Francelos House, Vila Nova de Gaia,
Portugal, 1980 (design)

Caixa Geral de Depósitos, Matosinhos,
Portugal, 1980 (design)

Monument to António Nobre,
Leça da Palmeira, Portugal, 1980

Housing at Charlottenburg, Berlin,
Germany, 1980 (design)

Teixeira Apartment, Póvoa de Varzim,
Portugal, 1980–84

Teixeira House, Taipas, Guimarães,
Portugal, 1980–88

Dom Headquarters, Cologne,
Germany, 1980 (design)

Apartment Building, Kottbusser
Damm, Berlin, Germany, 1980 (design)

Crédito Predial Bank, Montalegre,
Portugal, 1980 (design)

Avelino Duarte House, Ovar,
Portugal, 1980–84

Bonjour Tristesse Apartment
Building, Schlesisches Tor,
Berlin, Germany, 1980–84
(with P. Brinkert)

Ulli Böhme House,
Berlin, Germany, 1981

Fernando Machado House, Porto,
Portugal, 1981 (design)

Social Housing, Vila Viçosa,
Portugal, 1981 (design)

Social Housing, Aviz,
Portugal, 1981 (design)

Cultural Center, Sines,
Portugal, 1982–85 (design)

Urban Development Plan,
Guimãraes, Portugal, 1982

Guimarães da Costa House, Trofa,
Portugal, 1982 (design)

Mário Bahia House, Gondomar,
Portugal, 1983–

Nina Boutique, Porto, Portugal, 1983

Macao City Expansion Plan,
Macao, 1983–84 (with F. Távora)

Kulturforum, Berlin,
Germany, 1983 (design)

Salemi Church, Salemi, Sicily, Italy, 1983

Monument to Gestapo Victims,
Prinz Albrecht Palais, Berlin,
Germany, 1983 (design, competition)

Social Headquarters of Boa Vontade
Co-operative, Évora,
Portugal, 1983 (design)

Motel, Quinta da Malagueira,
Évora, Portugal, 1983–

Extension to the Institut Français,
Porto, Portugal, 1983 (design)

Urban Planning and Social Housing,
Delgebiet 5, Schilderswijk-West,
The Hague, The Netherlands, 1983–84

Social Housing, De Punkt en
de Komma, Schilderswijk-West,
The Hague, The Netherlands, 1983–88

Proposals for Caserta, Naples,
Italy, 1984 (design)

Vieira de Castro House,
Famalicão, Portugal, 1984–98

Erhard Josef Pascher House,
Sintra, Portugal, 1984 (design)

Luis Figueiredo House, Gondomar,
Portugal, 1984–94

"João de Deus" Kindergarten,
Penafiel, Portugal, 1984–91

Housing and Boutiques,
Schilderswijk-Centrum, The Hague,
The Netherlands, 1984–88

Van der Venne Park Garden,
Schilderswijk-West, The Hague,
The Netherlands, 1985–88

Giudecca Area Restoration,
Venice, Italy, 1985 (design)

Quinta da Espertina Housing Estate,
Águeda, Portugal, 1985 (design)

J. Oliveira e Filho Housing Estate,
Águeda, Portugal, 1985 (design)

Restoration of House and
Annex Quinta da Póvoa,
Faculty of Architecture, Porto,
Portugal, 1985–86

Carlos Ramos Pavilion,
Faculty of Architecture, Porto,
Portugal, 1985–86

Town Park, Salemi,
Sicily, Italy, 1986 (competition)

Restoration of Plan Cascio, Salemi,
Sicily, Italy, 1986–97 (with R. Collovà)

Hydrographic Institute, Lisbon,
Portugal, 1986 (design)

Extension to Casino and
Restaurant Winkler, Salzburg,
Austria, 1986 (design)

Expo '92 Master Plan,
Seville, Spain, 1986 (design)

City Block, Naples,
Italy, 1986–87

Competition for Monterusciello
Plan and Flegrei Field,
Trienal of Milan, Italy, 1986–87

Kindergarten, Schlesische Strasse,
Berlin, Germany, 1986–88
(with P. Brinkert)

Superior School of Education,
Setúbal, Portugal, 1986–94

Old Age Home, Falckensteinstrasse,
Berlin, Germany, 1987–88
(with P. Brinkert)

Faculty of Architecture of the University
of Porto, Porto, Portugal, 1987–93

César Rodrigues House,
Porto, Portugal, 1987–96

La Defensa Cultural Center,
Madrid, Spain, 1988 (competition)

"Un Progetto per Siena,"
Italy, 1988 (competition)

Water Reservoir,
Aveiro, Portugal, 1988–89

Library of the University of Aveiro,
Aveiro, Portugal, 1988–95

Galician Center for Contemporary Art,
Santiago de Compostela,
Spain, 1988–93

Sports Complex, Villanueva de Arosa,
Spain, 1988 (design)

Alcino Cardoso House (rural complex),
Moledo do Minho, Portugal, 1988–91

Guardiola House, Seville,
Spain, 1988 (design)

Carvalho Araújo Gallery, Lisbon,
Portugal, 1988–89

Remodeling of Miranda Santos House,
Matosinhos, Portugal, 1988–93

Reconstruction Plan for the Chiado
Area, Lisbon, Portugal, 1988–

Portal de Riquer, Alcoi-Valencia,
Spain, 1988–

Housing in Concepción Arenal,
Cádiz, Spain, 1989–

Competition for the Library of France,
Paris, France, 1989 (design)

Social Housing, Doedijnstraat,
Schilderswijk, The Hague,
The Netherlands, 1989–93

Praça de Espanha Master Plan and
Traffic Signals, Lisbon, Portugal, 1989–

Church and Parochial Center,
Malagueira, Évora,
Portugal, 1989– (design)

Santo Ovidio Estate, Douro Litoral,
Portugal, 1989–92 (first phase);
1997–2001 (second phase)

Office Buildings, Oliveira de Azeméis,
Portugal, 1989–95

> 1990-99 Ana Costa House, Lousada,
Portugal, 1990–

Pereira Ganhão House, Tróia,
Portugal, 1990 (design)

Santa Maria Church, Marco de
Canavezes, Portugal, 1990–96

Ceramique Terrain, Maastricht,
The Netherlands, 1990–

Santo Domingo de Bonaval
Restaurant, Santiago de Compostela,
Spain, 1990 (design)

Santo Domingo de Bonaval Garden,
Santiago de Compostela,
Spain, 1990–94

Olympic Village Meteorological Center,
Barcelona, Spain, 1990–92

Avenida José Malhoa Master Plan,
Lisbon, Portugal, 1990–92

Boulevard Brune Cité de la Jeunesse,
Paris, France, 1990 (competition)

Rectory and Law Library,
Nou Camp, University of Valencia,
Valencia, Spain, 1990–

Remodeling of Boa Nova Tea House
and Restaurant, Leça da Palmeira,
Portugal, 1991

Rua do Ouro, Massarelos, Porto,
Portugal, 1991 (design)

Boavista Tourism Complex, Porto,
Portugal, 1991– (with A. Madureira)

Boavista Building, Porto,
Portugal, 1991–98

Castro & Melo Building, Lisbon,
Portugal, 1991–94

Camara Chaves Building, Lisbon,
Portugal, 1991–96

Boavista Eurocenter, Porto,
Portugal, 1991 (design) (with A.
Madureira)

Vitra International Office Furniture
Factory, Weil am Rhein,
Germany, 1991–94

Restoration of Grandes Armazéns do
Chiado Building, Lisbon,
Portugal, 1991–

Grandella Building, Lisbon,
Portugal, 1991–96

"Pai Ramiro" Restaurant,
Porto, Portugal, 1991–

Rua do Arco de S. Mamede, Lisbon,
Portugal, 1991 (design)

Multimedia Institute, Journalism
Training Center and Contemporary
Performance Academy, Bouça,
Porto, Portugal, 1991 (design)

Málaga (Housing) Plan, Málaga,
Spain, 1992 (with M. Salgado)

Headquarters of the Young
Businessmen's Association, Oeiras,
Portugal, 1992–95 (with A. Madureira)

Condes Cinema, Lisbon,
Portugal, 1992

"Terraços de Bragança," Lisbon,
Portugal, 1995–2001

Headquarters of "25 de Abril"
Association, Lisbon,
Portugal, 1992–2001

Restaurant and Tea House,
Malagueira, Évora,
Portugal, 1992– (design)

Language Center, Malagueira, Évora,
Portugal, 1992– (design)

Baixa/Chiado Subway Station,
Lisbon, Portugal, 1992–98

"Visions for Madrid" Exhibition,
Madrid, Spain, 1992

Museum of Contemporary Art for
Helsinki, Finland, 1992–93
(competition) (with S. de Moura)

Headquarters of Lusitânia Insurance
Company, Lisbon, Portugal, 1993

São João Master Plan, Costa da
Caparica, Lisbon, Portugal, 1993–

Block of Flats, Setúbal,
Portugal, 1993 (design)

Block of Flats, Matosinhos,
Portugal, 1993 (design)

Restoration of the Ocean Swimming
Pool, Leça da Palmeira,
Portugal, 1993–95

Restaurant near the Ocean Swimming
Pool, Leça da Palmeira,
Portugal, 1993– (design)

Restoration of the Costa Braga
Building/Youth's House, Matosinhos,
Portugal, 1993–99

"Revigrés" Exhibition Hall, Águeda,
Portugal, 1993–97

Headquarters of the Cargaleiro
Foundation, Lisbon,
Portugal, 1993 (design)

Álvaro Siza Office, Évora,
Portugal, 1993

Álvaro Siza Office (and others), Porto,
Portugal, 1993–97

Two Houses, Teixeira da Cunha,
Felgueiras, Portugal, 1993 (design)

Plan "Centre Ville," Montreuil,
France, 1993 (design)

Housing, Montreuil,
France, 1993 (design)

Artists' Studio, Montreuil,
France, 1993 (design)

Laboratory, Showroom, Housing,
Venice, Italy, 1993

"The J. Paul Getty Museum"
Competition, Santa Monica, USA, 1993
(selected design)

Restaurant and Offices "Puerta Real,"
Granada, Spain, 1993–95 (design)

Faculty of Journalism,
Santiago de Compostela, Spain,
1993–2000

Social Housing "CasaJovem,"
Guarda, Portugal, 1994–

Children's Farm, Serralves Foundation,
Porto, Portugal, 1994

Granell Museum, Santiago de
Compostela, Spain, 1994– (design)

Parking of La Salle, Santiago de
Compostela, Spain, 1994 (design)

Restoration of Casa de Serralves,
Porto, Portugal, 1994

Fountain for Vitra International,
Weil am Rhein, Germany,
1994– (design)

Social Housing T1 and T4,
Malagueira, Évora, Portugal, 1994–

"João de Deus" Kindergarten Annex,
Penafiel, Portugal, 1994–

Rossio de São Brás Master Plan,
Évora, Portugal, 1994– (design)

Palma di Montechiaro Historic Center
Master Plan, Palma di Montechiaro,
Sicily, Italy, 1994– (design)

Remodeling of the ancient Market
"2 de Maio," Viseu,
Portugal, 1994– (design)

Remodeling of Elevador de Santa Justa,
Lisbon, Portugal, 1994– (design)

Competition for the Ishmaelite Center
and Aga Khan Foundation, Lisbon,
Portugal, 1995 (design) (with A.
Madureira)

Remodeling and Extension of
the Stedelijk Museum, Amsterdam,
The Netherlands, 1995– (design)

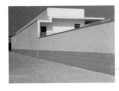

Universiades '97 Sports Complex,
Palermo, Sicily, Italy, 1995 (design)

Rectory of the University of Alicante,
Alicante, Spain, 1995

APDL-Harbour of Leixões
Administrative Building, Matosinhos,
Portugal, 1995–

Pinto da Sousa House, Oeiras,
Portugal, 1995– (design)

Plan for Lagoinha, Belo Horizonte,
Brazil, 1995– (design)

Plan and Restaurant for Involving
Zone, Guimarães,
Portugal, 1995– (design)

Town Hall of Caorle, Caorle,
Italy, 1995–

Housing Complex and Renovation of
Two Houses at "Quinta da Palmeira",
Évora, Portugal, 1995

Agostino Vieira House, Baião,
Portugal, 1995–

Pre-Primary and Primary Schools,
Alcoi, Alicante,
Spain, 1995– (design)

Biophysics Institute,
Hombroich Island, Neuss,
Germany, 1995– (design)

Fehlbaum Family Grave,
Weil am Rhein, Germany, 1995–96

Extension to Ritz Hotel, Lisbon,
Portugal, 1995 (with A. Madureira)

Portuguese Pavilion, Expo '98,
Lisbon, Portugal, 1995–98

Scenery Design for the Ballet
Presentation at Gulbenkian
Foundation, Lisbon, Portugal, 1996

Kolonihaven, Copenhagen,
Denmark, 1996 (design)

Competition for Metro of Porto,
Portugal, 1996 (design) (with A.
Madureira)

European Architects in Thessaloniki
(Capital of Culture 1997),
Thessaloniki, Greece, 1996 (design)

Revision Plan Matosinhos South,
Matosinhos, Portugal, 1996
(design) (with A. Madureira)

Clinic, Malagueira, Évora,
Portugal, 1996 (design)

Mixed Complex in "Rotunda do
Raimundo", Évora, Portugal, 1996

Serralves Foundation, Porto,
Portugal, 1996–99

New Beer Hall, Chiado,
Lisbon, Portugal, 1997 (design)

Urban Park and Activities Centre,
Caxinas, Vila do Conde, Portugal, 1997
(design)

Cultural Center "Manzana del
Revellín," Ceuta, Spain, 1997

Hotel, Almeria,
Spain, 1997

Sports Pavilion, Vigo, Portugal, 1997
(design) (with R. Collovà)

Plan for a Square and Buildings,
Felgueiras, Portugal, 1997

Municipal Center in the South District,
Rosario, Argentina, 1997

Board Building and Auditorium, Nou
Camp, Valencia University, Spain, 1997

"Renova" Paper Factory
and Showroom, Torres Novas,
Portugal, 1997

Restoration of a Café,
Pontevedra, Portugal, 1997

Van Middelem-Dupont House,
Oudenburg, Belgium, 1997–2001

Villa Colonnese, Vicenza,
Italy, 1998 (design)

Carcereira Mixed Complex, Porto,
Portugal, 1998 (with A. Madureira)

Mixed Complex "Zaida Building,"
Granada, Spain, 1998
(with J. Domingo)

Plan for Cidade Velha, Cape Verde,
1998

Cape Verde National Bank,
Cape Verde, 1998

Building for Hotel and Housing in Vila
do Conde, Portugal, 1998

Cultural Centre and Auditorium for the
Iberê Camargo Foundation, Porto
Alegre, Brazil, 1998 (competition)

Library at the University of Salamanca,
Salamanca, Spain, 1998

Headquarters of the Municipality
of Penafiel, Portugal, 1998

Adaptation of the Pavilion of Portugal to Ministers Council, Parque das Nações, Lisbon, Portugal, 1999

Museum of Architecture, Matosinhos, Portugal, 1999

Restoration of the Solar de Magalhães for Rei Afonso Henriques Foundation, Amarante, Portugal, 1999

Millenium Park, Maia, Portugal, 1999

Júlio House, Vila do Conde, Portugal, 1999

Banif Building, Funchal, Madeira Island, Portugal, 1999

Portuguese Pavilion, Expo 2000, Hanover, Germany, 1999 (with Souto Moura)

Ordenación del Parque de Tenes, Parets del Vallès, Barcelona, Spain, 1999

Plan for Vapor Turull, Sabadell, Barcelona, Spain, 1999

Library of Town Hall of Albergaria-a-Velha, Portugal, 1999

Paço da Giela, Arcos de Valdevez, Portugal, 1999

Initial design for the Room of Pietà Rondanini, Castello Sforzesco, Milan, Italy, 1999 (competition – 1st prize)

> 2000- House Recuperation of Serralves Foundation, Porto, Portugal, 2000–

Porto 2001 – Plan for Avenida D. Afonso Henriques (Av. da Ponte), Porto, Portugal, 2000

Porto 2001 – Landscaping project for Praça da Liberdade, Porto, Portugal, 2000

Porto 2001 – Cativo Fountain, Porto, Portugal, 2000

Pavilion, Gondomar, Portugal, 2000 (design)

Atlantic Park, Vila de Conde, Portugal, 2000–

Peniche Lodging-House, 2000–

Villa Zileri, Vicenza, Italy, 2000

Marginal Avenue, Vila de Conde, Portugal, 2000–

Manuel Cargaleiro II Foundation, Seixal, Portugal, 2000

Séquia de Manresa Park, Barcelona, Spain, 2000

Library of Town Hall, Viana do Castelo, Portugal, 2000

Camping Park, Mont-Roig del Camp, Tarragona, Portugal, 2001

Portal Farm, Sabrosa, Portugal, 2001

Art Center College of Design, Pasadena, USA, 2001

David Rosas Jewellery, Lisbon, Portugal, 2001–2002

25 Years Anniversary Monument, Coimbra, Portugal, 2001–2002

Reconstruction of the Portuguese Pavilion for the Expo 2000 in Coimbra, Portugal, 2001–2003

Plan for Principe Isle, St. Tomé and Principe, 2001–

House in Palma de Majorca, Spain, 2001–

Special Plan Recoletos-Prado, Madrid, Spain, 2002 (competition)

Armanda Passos House, Porto, Portugal, 2002

Saramago Foundation, Granada, Spain, 2002

Carlos Alemão House, Sintra, Portugal, 2002–

"Caja Rural" Bank (Zaida Building), Granada, Spain, 2002–

Housing Complex New Orleans, Rotterdam, The Netherlands, 2002–

Santa Maria Church, Parish Center Marco de Canavezes, Portugal, 2003–

Biography

_Álvaro Joaquim Melo Siza Vieira was born in Matosinhos (near Porto) in 1933. From 1949-55 he studied at the School of Architecture, University of Porto (ESBAP). His first built project was finished in 1954.
_From 1955-58 he was collaborator of Arch. Fernando Távora. He taught at the ESBAP from 1966-69 and was appointed Professor of Construction in 1976.
_He has been a Visiting Professor at the École Polytechnique Fédérale of Lausanne, the University of Pennsylvania, Los Andes University of Bogotá and the Graduate School of Design of Harvard University in Cambridge; he continues to teach at the School of Architecture of Porto.
_He is the architect of more than one hundred-fifty buildings and projects.
_His works have been exhibited in: Copenhagen (1975); Aarhus and Barcelona (1976); Biennale of Venice (1978); Milan (1979); Museum of Finnish Architecture, Helsinki, Alvar Aalto Museum, Jyväskylä, and Centre Georges Pompidou, Paris (1982); Institute of Contemporary Arts, London, and Stichting Wonen, Amsterdam (1983); Technische Hogeschool, Delft, ESBAP, Porto, and Almada Negreiros Gallery, Lisbon (1984); International Building Exhibition, Berlin (1984 and 1987); Biennale of Paris and Massachusetts Institute of Technology, Cambridge (1985); 9H Gallery, London (1986); Columbia University, New York (1987); Harvard Graduate School of Design, Cambridge (1988); Centre Georges Pompidou, Paris, and MOPU Gallery/Ministerio de Obras Publicas, Madrid (1990); Royal Institute of British Architects (RIBA), London, and Colegio de Arquitectos, Sevilla (1991); deSingel Gallery, Antwerp (1992); Rui Alberto Gallery, Porto, MOPU, Madrid, GA Gallery, Tokyo, and Biennale of São Paulo (1993); Colegio de Arquitectos, Granada and Seville, and Sala do Risco, Lisbon (1994); Centro Galego de Arte Contemporanea, Santiago de Compostela, Antico Convento de Santa Clara, Republic of San Marino, Società Ticinese di Belle Arti, Mendrisio/Comune di Como (1995); Gammeldok, Copenhagen, Municipality of Matosinhos, Belém Cultural Centre, Lisbon, and Colegio de Arquitectos, Tenerife (1996); Fondation pour l'Architecture, Brussels (1997); Fundación ICO (sculpture), Madrid (1998); Basilica Palladiana, Vicenza (1999).
_He has participated in numerous lectures and conferences in Portugal, Spain, Italy, Germany, France, Norway, Holland, Switzerland, Austria, England, Colombia, Argentina, Brazil, Japan, Canada and United States.
_Having been invited to participate in international competitions, he won the first place in Schlesisches Tor, Kreuzberg, Berlin (1980), at the recuperation of Campo di Marte in Venice (1985) and at the renewal of Casino and Café Winkler, Salzburg (1986). He has participated in the competitions for Expo '92 in Sevilla (1986), for "Un Progetto per Siena" (1988), and for the Cultural Centre La Defensa in Madrid (1988/89), being the winner of the latter; and also for the Bibliothèque de France in Paris (1989/90), the Helsinki Museum (1993) and the Islamic Centre in Lisbon (1994). He was the winner of the competitions for the exhibition room of Pietà Rondanini in the Museo del Castello Sforzesco, Milan (1999), and for Paseo del Prado/Paseo de Recoletos in Madrid (2002).
_The Portuguese Department of the International Association of Art Critics awarded him the Prize of Architecture of 1982. He received an Award from the Portuguese Architects Association in 1987. In 1988 he was awarded the Gold Medal of the Colegio de Architectos, Spain, the Gold Medal of the Alvar Aalto Foundation, the Prince of Wales Prize in Urban Design by Harvard University and the European Award of Architecture by the Economic European Comunity/Mies van der Rohe Foundation, Barcelona. In 1992 he was awarded the Pritzker Prize by the Hyatt Foundation of Chicago for his entire work. In 1993 the Portuguese Architects Association gave him the National Prize of Architecture. In 1994 he received the Dr. H. P. Berlagestichting Prize and the Gubbio Prize/Associazione Nazionale Centri Storico-Artistici. In 1995 the Nara World Architecture Exposition awarded him the Gold Medal; and the Fiera di Verona gave him the International Award Architetture di Pietra. In 1996 he was awarded the Secil Prize of Architecture, and in 1997 the Manuel de la Dehesa Award by the Menendez Pelayo University, in Santander. In 1998 he received the Arnold W. Brunner Memorial Prize by the American Academy of Arts and Letters, New York; the Premio IberFAD de Arquitectura by the Fomento de las Artes Decorativas, Barcelona; and the Praemium Imperiale by the Japan Art Association, Tokyo, and the Gold Medal by the Circulo de Bellas Artes of Madrid. In 1999 he received the Grã-Cruz da Ordem do Infante D. Henrique given by the Presidency of the Portuguese Republic, and the Leca Prize of Construction '98. In 2000, the Fondazione Frate Sole in Pavia gave him the Premio Internazionale di Architettura Sacra. In 2001 he was awarded the Wolf Prize in Arts by The Wolf Foundation in Israel and Alexandre Herculano National Architecture Prize.
_Doctor honoris causa by University of Valencia (1992), by École Polytéchnique Fédérale of Lausanne (1993), by the Palermo University (1995), by Menendez Pelayo University in Santander (1995), by the Universidad Nacional de Ingeniería de Lima (1995), by the University of Coimbra (1997), by the Universidade Lusíada (1999), and by Paraíba Federal University (2000).
_He is member of the American Academy of Arts and Science, Honorary Fellow of the Royal Institute of British Architects, AIA/American Institute of Architects, Académie d'Architecture de France and European Academy of Sciences and Arts.

_Álvaro Joaquim Melo Siza Vieira naît à Matosinhos, dans la banlieue de Porto, en 1933. De 1949 à 1955, il étudie l'architecture à l'Escola Superior de Belas Artes de Porto (ESBAP) et ses premières réalisations voient le jour en 1954.

_De 1955 à 1958, il travaille avec l'architecte Fernando Távora. De 1966 à 1969, il enseigne à l'ESBAP, où il sera nommé professeur assistant en construction en 1976.

_Il a été professeur invité à l'École Polytechnique Fédérale de Lausanne, à l'Université de Pennsylvanie, l'Université Los Andes à Bogotá et la Graduate School of Design de Harvard University à Cambridge. Il enseigne toujours à l'ESBAP de Porto.

_Il a signé plus de 150 réalisations et projets.

_Ses œuvres ont fait l'objet d'expositions dans le monde entier: Copenhague (1975); Arhus et Barcelone (1976); Biennale de Venise (1978); Milan (1979); Musée d'architecture, Helsinki, Musée Alvar Aalto, Jyväskylä, et Centre Georges Pompidou, Paris (1982); Institute of Contemporary Arts, Londres, et Stichting Wonen, Amsterdam (1983); Technische Hogeschool, Delft, ESBAP, Porto, et Galerie Almada Negreiros, Lisbonne (1984); Internationale Bauausstellung (IBA), Berlin (1984 et 1987); Biennale de Paris et Massachusetts Institute of Technology, Cambridge (1985); 9H Gallery, Londres (1986); Columbia University, New York (1987); Harvard Graduate School of Design, Cambridge (1988); Centre Georges Pompidou, Paris, et Galerie MOPU/Ministère des Travaux publics, Madrid (1990); Royal Institute of British Architects (RIBA), Londres, et Colegio de Arquitectos, Séville (1991); galerie deSingel, Anvers (1992); galerie Rui Alberto, Porto, MOPU, Madrid, GA Gallery, Tokyo, et Biennale de São Paulo (1993); Colegio de Arquitectos, Grenade et Séville, et Sala do Risco, Lisbonne (1994); Centro Galego de Arte Contemporanea, Saint-Jacques de Compostelle, Antico Convento de Santa Clara, République de Saint-Marin, Società Ticinese di Belle Arti, Mendrisio/Côme (1995); Gammeldock, Copenhague, municipalité de Matosinhos, Centre culturel de Belém, Lisbonne, et Colegio de Arquitectos, Tenerife (1996); Fondation pour l'Architecture, Bruxelles (1997). Fundación ICO (Sculpture), Madrid (1998); Basilica Palladiana, Vicenza (1999).

_Siza a participé à de nombreux symposiums au Portugal, en Espagne, Italie, Allemagne, France, Norvège, aux Pays-Bas, en Suisse, Autriche, Grande-Bretagne, Colombie, Argentine, Brésil, Japon, Canada et aux États-Unis.

_Invité à participer à de nombreux concours internationaux, Siza a remporté les premiers prix suivants: pour la construction d'habitations Schlesisches Tor, Kreuzberg, Berlin (1980), la restauration du Campo di Marte à Venise (1985), et la restructuration du Casino et du café Winkler à Salzbourg (1986). Il a participé aux concours pour Expo '92 à Séville (1986), pour «Un progetto per Siena» (1988), pour le Centre culturel La Defensa à Madrid (1988/89), qu'il remporte, pour la Bibliothèque de France, Paris (1989/90), le Musée d'art contemporain d'Helsinki (1993), et le Centre islamique de Lisbonne (1994). Il a gagné le concours pour la réalisation de la salle d'exposition de la Pietà Rondanini au Museo del Castello Sforzesco, Milan (1999), et pour le Paseo del Prado/Paseo de Recoletos à Madrid (2002).

_La section portugaise de l' Association internationale des critiques d'art lui a remis son prix d'architecture en 1982. Il reçoit en 1987 un prix de l'Association des architectes portugais, et en 1988, la médaille d'or d'architecture du Colegio de Arquitectos (Espagne), la médaille d'or de la Fondation Alvar Aalto, le Prix Prince of Wales d'urbanisme de Harvard University, et le Prix européen d'architecture de la Fondation Mies van der Rohe et de la CEE à Barcelone. En 1992, il se voit accorder le Prix Pritzker par la Hyatt Foundation de Chicago pour l'ensemble de son œuvre. En 1993, il reçoit le prix national d'architecture de l'Association des architectes portugais, et en 1994, le prix de la Dr. H. P. Berlagestichting et le Prix Gubbio/Associazione Nazionale Centri Storico-artistici. En 1995, la Nara World Architecture Exhibition lui remet sa médaille d'or; et la Fiera di Verona le prix international Architteture di Pietra. En 1996, lui est

attribué le Secil Prize of Architecture, et, en 1977, le Prix Manuel de la Dehesa de l'Université Menendez Pelayo à Santander. En 1998, il reçoit le Prix Arnold W. Brunner Memorial de l'American Academy of Arts and Letters, New York, le Premio IberFAD de Arquitectura du Fomento de las Artes Decorativas, Barcelone, ainsi que le Praemium Imperiale de l'Association japonaise pour les Arts, Tokyo, et la médaille d'or du Circulo de Bellas Artes, Madrid. En 1999, il reçoit le Grã-Cruz da Ordem do Infante D. Henrique des mains du Président de la République du Portugal, et le Prix Leca pour Construction '98. En 2000, il se voit décerner le Premio Internazionale di Architettura Sacra par la Fondazione Frate Sole à Pavie, et en 2001 le Prix Wolf de la Wolf Foundation d'Israel ainsi que le Alexandre Herculano National Architecture Prize.

_Il est fait docteur honoris causa de l'Université de Valencia (1992), de l'École Polytechnique Fédérale de Lausanne (1993), de l'Université de Palerme (1995), de l'Université Menendez Pelayo de Santander (1995), de la Universidad Nacional de Ingeniería de Lima (1995), de l'Université de Coimbra (1997), de la Universidade Lusíada (1999) et de l'Université Fédérale Paraíba (2000).

_Il est membre de l 'Académie des Arts et des Sciences américaine, est Honorary Fellow du Royal Institute of British Architects, du AIA/American Institute of Architects, de l'Académie d'Architecture de France et de l'Académie européenne des Sciences et des Arts.

Biographie

_Álvaro Joaquim Melo Siza Vieira wurde 1933 in Matosinhos (bei Porto), Portugal, geboren. Von 1949–55 studierte er Architektur an der Escola Superior de Belas Artes (ESBAP) in Porto. Die erste Realisierung eines seiner Entwürfe wurde 1954 abgeschlossen.

_Von 1955–58 arbeitete Siza mit dem Architekten Fernando Távora zusammen. Von 1966–69 war er Dozent an der ESBAP und wurde 1976 zum Professor für Konstruktion berufen.

_Er war Gastprofessor an der École Polytechnique Fédérale von Lausanne, der University of Pennsylvania, der Los Andes-Universität in Bogotá und an der Graduate School of Design der Harvard University in Cambridge. Er lehrt weiterhin an der ESBAP in Porto.

_Sein Werk umfasst über 150 Bauten und Projekte.

_Seine Arbeiten sind in Ausstellungen in vielen Ländern gezeigt worden: Kopenhagen (1975); Arhus und Barcelona (1976); Biennale in Venedig (1978); Mailand (1979); Museum für Finnische Architektur, Helsinki, Alvar-Aalto-Museum, Jyväskylä, und Centre Georges Pompidou, Paris (1982); Institute of Contemporary Arts, London, und Stichting Wonen, Amsterdam (1983); Technische Hogeschool, Delft, ESBAP, Porto, und Galeria Almada Negreiros, Lissabon (1984); Internationale Bauausstellung (IBA), Berlin (1984 und 1987); Pariser Biennale und Massachusetts Institute of Technology, Cambridge (1985); 9H Gallery, London (1986); Columbia University, New York (1987); Harvard Graduate School of Design, Cambridge (1988); Centre Georges Pompidou, Paris, und MOPU-Galerie, Bauministerium Madrid (1990); Royal Institute of British Architects (RIBA), London, und Colegio de Arquitectos, Sevilla (1991); deSingel, Antwerpen (1992); Galerie Rui Alberto, Porto, MOPU, Madrid, GA Gallery, Tokio, und Biennale von São Paulo (1993); Colegio de Arquitectos, Granada und Sevilla, und Sala do Risco, Lissabon (1994); Centro Galego de Arte Contemporanea, Santiago de Compostela, Antico Convento de Santa Clara, Republik San Marino, Società Ticinese di Belle Arti, Mendrisio/Como (1995); Gammeldok, Kopenhagen, Gemeindezentrum von Matosinhos, Belém-Kulturzentrum, Lissabon, und Colegio de Arquitectos, Teneriffa (1996); Fondation pour l'Architecture, Brüssel (1997); Fundación ICO (Skulptur), Madrid (1998); Basilica Palladiana, Vicenza (1999).

_Siza hat zahlreiche Vorträge gehalten und an Symposien teilgenommen in Portugal, Spanien, Italien, Deutschland, Frankreich, Norwegen, den Niederlanden, der Schweiz, Österreich, Großbritannien, Kolumbien, Argentinien, Brasilien, Japan, Kanada und den Vereinigten Staaten.

_Als eingeladener Teilnehmer an internationalen Architekturwettbewerben gewann Siza erste Preise für folgende Entwürfe: Wohnbebauung Schlesisches Tor, Berlin (1980), Restaurierung des Campo di Marte, Venedig (1985), sowie Um- und Neubau des Casino und Café Winkler, Salzburg (1986). Er beteiligte sich an den Wettbewerben für die Expo '92 in Sevilla (1986), für »Un Progetto per Siena« (1988), für das Kulturzentrum La Defensa in Madrid (1988/89) – aus dem er als Sieger hervorging –, die Bibliothèque de France in Paris (1989/90), das Museum für zeitgenössische Kunst in Helsinki (1993) und das Islamische Zentrum, Lissabon (1994). Er hat die Wettbewerbe um die Gestaltung des Ausstellungsraums der Pietà Rondanini im Museo del Castello Sforzesco, Mailand, gewonnen (1999) und für den Paseo del Prado/Paseo de Recoletos in Madrid (2002).

_Die portugiesische Sektion des Internationalen Kunstkritikerverbands verlieh Siza ihren Architekturpreis 1982. Außerdem erhielt er 1987 eine Auszeichnung des portugiesischen Architektenverbands. 1988 erhielt er die Goldmedaille für Architektur vom Colegio de Arquitectos, Spanien, die Goldmedaille der Alvar-Aalto-Stiftung, den Prince-of-Wales-Preis für Städtebau der Harvard University und den Europäischen Architekturpreis, der von der Europäischen Kommission und der Mies-van-der-Rohe-Stiftung, Barcelona, verliehen wird. 1992 erhielt er von der Hyatt Foundation, Chicago, den Pritzker-Preis für sein Gesamtwerk und 1993 den Nationalen Architekturpreis des portugiesischen Architektenverbands. 1994 erhielt er den Preis der Dr. H. P. Berlagestichting und den Gubbio-Preis der Associazione Nazionale Centri Storico-Artistici. 1995 verlieh ihm die Nara World Architecture Exposition die Goldmedaille, und im selben Jahr erhielt er anlässlich der Fiera di Verona den Internationalen Preis Architetture di Pietra. 1996 wurde Siza mit dem Secil Prize of Architecture ausgezeichnet und 1997 mit dem Manuel-de-la-Dehesa-Preis der Menendez-Pelayo-Universität in Santander. 1998 erhielt er von der American Academy of Arts and Letters, New York, den Arnold-W.-Brunner-Memorial-Preis, den Premio IberFAD de Arquitectura des Fomento de las Artes Decorativas, Barcelona, von der Japan Art Association in Tokio den Praemium Imperiale und die Goldmedaille des Circulo de Bellas Artes, Madrid. 1999 erhielt er den Grã-Cruz da Ordem do Infante D. Henrique vom Präsidenten der Republik Portugal, und den Leca-Preis für Konstruktion '98. Im Jahr 2000 wurde ihm von der Fondazione Frate Sole in Pavia der Premio Internazionale di Architettura Sacra zuerkannt, 2001 der Wolf-Preis der Wolf Foundation in Israel und der Alexandre Herculano National Architecture Prize.

_Die Universität Valencia verlieh ihm den Ehrendoktortitel (1992), ebenso die École Polytechnique Fédérale in Lausanne (1993), die Universität in Palermo (1995), die Menendez-Pelayo-Universität in Santander (1995), die Universidad Nacional de Ingeniería in Lima (1995), die Universität in Coimbra (1997), die Universidade Lusíada (1999) und die Paraíba-Universität.

_Er ist Mitglied der amerikanischen Academy of Arts and Science, Honorary Fellow des Royal Institute of British Architects, des AIA/American Institute of Architects, der Académie d'Architecture de France und der Europäischen Akademie der Wissenschaften und Künste.

Bibliography > Bibliographie

Alvar Aalto, Between Humanism and Materialism. The Museum of Modern Art, New York, 1998.

"Álvaro Siza 1958–1994,"
El Croquis, n° 68/69.
El Croquis Editorial, Madrid, 1994.

"Centre galicien d'art contemporain,"
L'Architecture d'Aujourd'hui, 1994.

GA Document 50,
ADA Edita, Tokyo, 1997.

dos Santos, José Paulo (ed.):
Álvaro Siza, Works & Projects 1954–1992.
Editorial Gustavo Gili, Barcelona, 1993.

*Edouardo Souto de Moura,
Recent Work.* 2G, n° 5, 1998,
Editorial Gustavo Gili, Barcelona.

Trigueiros, Luiz (ed.): *Álvaro Siza
1986–1995.* Editorial Blau,
Lisbon, 1995.

Trigueiros, Luiz (ed.): *Álvaro Siza
1954–1976.* Editorial Blau,
Lisbon, 1997.

Photographic credits > Crédits photographiques > Fotonachweis